MOON

COPÁN

AMY E. ROBERTSON

Contents

Copán and Western Honduras 4
Planning Your Time 7
History 8

Copán Ruinas Town 9
Sights............................ 11
Entertainment......................12
Shopping..........................12
Accommodations 12
Food..............................17
Information and Services..........18
Getting There and Away............19
Getting Around 20
Near Copán Ruinas Town 21

The Ruins of Copán.......... 24
History of the Mayan City of Copán 24
Exploring the Ruins of Copán...................... 26
Museo de Escultura Maya........... 35

La Entrada and the Ruins of El Puente 36
La Entrada 36
El Puente........................ 36

Santa Rosa de Copán 37
Sights........................... 39
Entertainment.................... 40
Shopping......................... 42
Accommodations 42
Food............................. 43
Information and Services.......... 45
Getting There and Around 45
Near Santa Rosa de Copán.......... 46

Gracias and the Lenca Highlands.......... 48
Gracias 48
Parque Nacional Celaque 57
Lenca Villages South of Gracias.................. 60
San Juan......................... 65
La Esperanza..................... 68

Ocotepeque 76
Accommodations 76
Food.............................76
Information and Services..........77
Getting There and Away............77
Near Ocotepeque 78

COPÁN

© AMY E. ROBERTSON

COPÁN AND WESTERN HONDURAS

Intricately carved Mayan ruins, tiny Lencan villages, impressive cloud forest, and the country's highest mountain are all within this region, but it draws only a fraction of the tourists that flock to similar attractions in neighboring countries. Just a few miles from the Guatemalan border, the ruins of Copán are a must-see for visitors to Honduras. Built by a society of scientists and architects, artists and warriors, the ruins boast stelae (carved statues) and layers of temples, a ball court, and the famed Hieroglyphic Stairway, the longest hieroglyphic inscription found anywhere in the Americas. More than a millennium old, the ruins have been well preserved, in part thanks to their isolation. In the hills around Copán are the villages of Chortí Maya, a people related to their highland cousins to the northwest in Guatemala.

An hour away is Santa Rosa de Copán, with its cobblestone streets, colonial buildings, and renowned cigar factory. Those whose visit coincides with Semana Santa will have the chance to observe the centuries-old traditions of colorful sawdust carpets over which solemn processions march, while visitors in the month of August will be treated to special festivities in honor of the town's patron saint.

Travels farther south are well worth the effort, taking visitors farther off the beaten path. This is Lenca territory, the land of Lempira, a famed Indian chief who battled the conquistadors to a standstill before being tricked and

© HUMBERTO KLUCK

HIGHLIGHTS

◖ **Coffee Plantations:** Whether you want to spend half a day or four, the *fincas* near Copán provide a relaxing getaway replete with birdwatching and horseback rides, as well as an education on the world's most popular beverage (page 22).

◖ **Exploring the Ruins of Copán:** The Mayan city of Copán is justifiably the top tourist destination in mainland Honduras, known as the Athens of Mesoamerica for its carved artwork and the detailed city history inscribed on its monuments (page 26).

◖ **Museo de Escultura Maya:** Journey through the serpent's jaws into the Maya Sculpture Museum, which houses a spectacular replica of the Rosalila Temple in all its Technicolor glory, along with the originals of many of the finest stelae and carvings from the ruins of Copán (page 35).

◖ **Feria Agostina:** A quiet colonial town most of the year, Santa Rosa bursts to life during its August *feria*, when *copanecos* celebrate their patron saint with music, food, sporting competitions, and even a Noche de Fumadores, an evening dedicated to fine cigars, and the Tarde con Aroma a Café, an afternoon tasting locally grown coffee (page 40).

◖ **Gracias:** This was once (briefly) the capital of Spanish Central America, but nowadays it's a sleepy little cowboy town with several beautiful colonial buildings and a newly renovated central park, and it is fast becoming a popular offbeat tourist destination (page 48).

◖ **Parque Nacional Celaque:** Even a short walk near the base of Celaque mountain can reveal the shy quetzal, while the stiff hike up the trail to the top of the country's highest mountain is well worth it for the fine cloud forest. You can soak your bones in the steaming *aguas termales* (hot springs) near Gracias when you're done (page 57).

◖ **Lenca Villages South of Gracias:** These villages are set amid some of the most picturesque mountain countryside in Central America, and they boast imposing 18th-century churches. La Campa and San Manuel Colohete are perfect places to hike for an hour, a day, or a week (page 60).

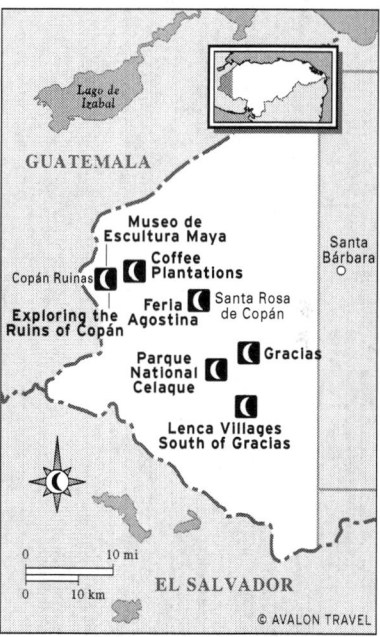

LOOK FOR ◖ TO FIND RECOMMENDED SIGHTS, ACTIVITIES, DINING, AND LODGING.

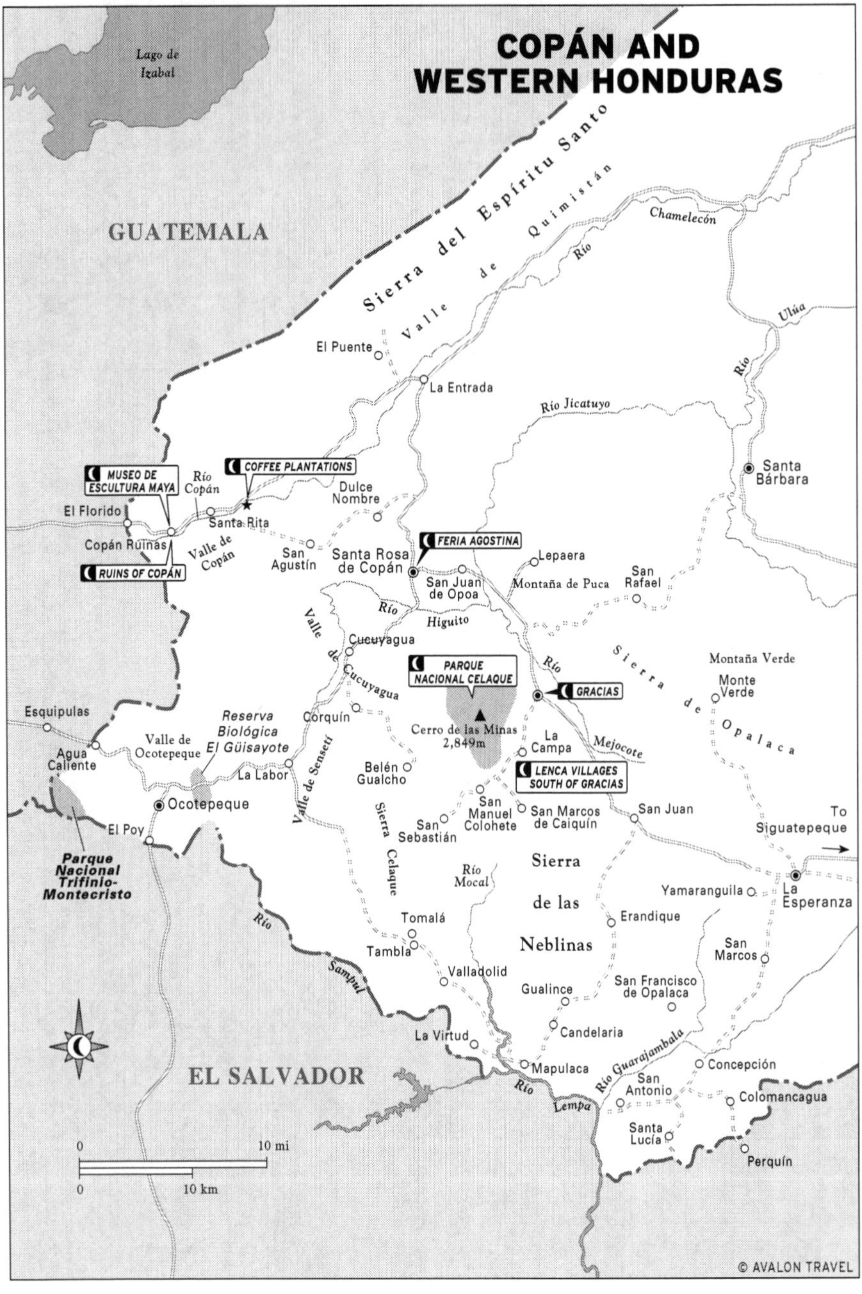
COPÁN AND WESTERN HONDURAS
Lago de Izabal
GUATEMALA
Sierra del Espíritu Santo
Valle de Quimistán
Río Chamelecón
Río Ulúa
El Puente
La Entrada
Río Jicatuyo
Santa Bárbara
MUSEO DE ESCULTURA MAYA
COFFEE PLANTATIONS
Río Copán
Dulce Nombre
El Florido
Santa Rita
Copán Ruinas
RUINS OF COPÁN
Valle de Copán
San Agustín
FERIA AGOSTINA
Santa Rosa de Copán
San Juan de Opoa
Lepaera
Montaña de Puca
San Rafael
Río Higuito
Valle de Cucuyagua
Cucuyagua
PARQUE NACIONAL CELAQUE
GRACIAS
Río Mejocote
Sierra de Opalaca
Montaña Verde
Monte Verde
Esquipulas
Agua Caliente
Valle de Ocotepeque
Reserva Biológica El Güisayote
Corquín
Cerro de las Minas 2,849m
La Campa
LENCA VILLAGES SOUTH OF GRACIAS
La Labor
Valle de Sensetí
Belén Gualcho
Ocotepeque
El Poy
San Sebastián
San Manuel Colohete
San Marcos de Caiquín
San Juan
To Siguatepeque
Sierra Celaque
Parque Nacional Trifinio-Montecristo
Río Mocal
Sierra de las Neblinas
Yamaranguila
La Esperanza
Río Sampul
Tomalá
Tambla
Erandique
San Marcos
Valladolid
Gualince
San Francisco de Opalaca
Candelaria
La Virtud
Mapulaca
Concepción
Río Guarajambala
EL SALVADOR
Río Lempa
San Antonio
Colomancagua
Santa Lucía
Perquín
0 10 mi
0 10 km
© AVALON TRAVEL

killed, and for whom the national currency is named. This is one of the most naturally beautiful and least explored areas in all of Central America. Here, the adventurous can lose themselves for weeks, traveling the mountain roads and footpaths between the colonial town of Gracias and remote villages like Erandique, La Campa, and Belén Gualcho, or climbing to the cloud forests of Sierra de Celaque, which boasts Honduras's highest peak, Cerro de las Minas, which reaches 2,849 meters (9,347 feet).

While tourist services exist in a number of spots—Copán Ruinas, Gracias, Santa Rosa de Copán, San Juan, La Esperanza—there are many untouched areas where the lack of creature comforts is more than compensated for by the thrill of visiting lovely villages seemingly lost in the mists of history, where locals may not know quite what to think of a passing foreigner but will invariably invite him or her in for a cup of strong black coffee and a chat.

Much of the mountainous region is still covered with *ocote* pine forest, mixed in with oak and liquidambar (sweet gum) at higher elevations and cloud forest on the peaks, although deforestation is a serious problem in many areas, as campesinos (peasants) cut wood for fuel or to clear more farm or grazing land.

The rainiest months in western Honduras are June, August, and September, but wet weather can hit at any time in the mountains. If you're planning on camping, come prepared to get wet. The temperature is normally quite comfortable—warm in the daytime and pleasantly cool at night—although it can get downright cold in La Esperanza and surrounding hills.

PLANNING YOUR TIME

While a visit to the primary ruin site at Copán takes just a couple of hours, it takes three full days to do justice to the region, with its multiple Mayan sites, hot baths, coffee farms, and other tourist attractions. The real Mayan buff will want to spend another day or two to see the smaller city of El Puente, near La Entrada, and less-frequented sites in the hills surrounding Copán.

It's easy to become seduced by this beguiling region of scenic mountains and friendly countryfolk, and want to see more than Copán. The town of Gracias is a good jumping-off point for hikes in the cloud forests of Parque Nacional Celaque and explorations of the nearby Lencan villages. A cursory visit to admire Gracias's colonial architecture, visit a couple of the nearby villages, and take a short hike at Celaque can be made with just a couple of days. Those with more time can summit Celaque in a two-day trip, hike the footpaths between the villages of La Campa and San Manuel Colohete, or spend a couple of days or more exploring the far-flung villages past Gracias toward El Salvador, like Erandique or San Juan.

Santa Rosa de Copán is the capital of the department of Copán and the unofficial capital of western Honduras. Although it doesn't boast much in the way of tourist attractions, it's a pleasant colonial town with good restaurants and hotels, and a convenient base for transport. (The town's one shortcoming might be its traffic, due to the narrowness of those colonial streets.) Holy Week (the week leading up to Easter) and during the patron saint festival in late August are especially good times to visit.

The main overland travel transport route into western Honduras from Guatemala is via Copán. Those who come in by Nueva Ocotepeque, from either Guatemala or El Salvador, should consider taking an extra day to hike into Reserva Biológica El Güisayote.

Guide Companies

Most of the destinations in western Honduras can be visited without guides. However, several companies offer more specialized trips that may appeal to some travelers.

In Copán Ruinas, **Basecamp** (tel. 504/2651-4695, www.basecamphonduras.com) and **Yaragua Tours** (tel. 504/2651-4147, www.

yaragua.com) offer a variety of adventuresome tours, including hikes and visits to the hot springs or a coffee plantation. The **Asociación de Guías Copán** (tel. 504/2651-4018, http://asociacionguiascopan.com), with its office right at the ruins, has guides who specialize in archaeology, history, nature, and even shamanism, and who can speak Spanish, English, French, and Italian (German too, if guide Antonio Ríos is around).

Max Elvir, a tireless promoter of tourism in western Honduras, runs **Lenca Travel** (tel. 504/9997-5340, lencatours@gmail.com or max@lenca-honduras.com) in Santa Rosa, offering tours of surrounding villages and natural areas, including Celaque, Monte Quetzal, and Belén Gualcho; farther afield to Celaque, Gracias, La Campa, San Juan, and Erandique; and any other place you might want to visit. Max works exclusively with small groups, and his tours are all customized to the interests of the traveler, and can even include learning about medicinal plants or a culinary class if the visitor is so inclined. A day tour to Belén Gualcho, Corquín, and an organic coffee farm runs US$25 per person for a group of four or more. If you have your own wheels, Max charges US$75 a day for guiding services. There is also an association of guides that can be contacted through **Santa Rosa's tourism office** (tel. 504/2630-1249, www.todocopan.com), but these should be booked in advance, as many have other jobs as well.

In Gracias, an excellent **community tourism network** has been developed. Extensive information on the region can be found on the website www.colosuca.com, and the **Asociación de Guías Turísticos Colosuca-Celaque** can do city tours, countryside tours, national park tours, or any combination thereof. The association's co-ordinator is Marco Aurelio Rodríguez (tel. 504/2656-0627 or 504/9870-8821, guiamarcolencas@yahoo.com).

HISTORY

By all accounts, western Honduras was densely populated by different indigenous groups, but archaeologists disagree on exactly which ones. Evidence from the Spanish suggests the people currently known as Lenca were at least a half-dozen distinct tribes during colonial times, including the Potón, Guaquí, Cares, Chatos, Dules, Paracas, and Yaras, who lived in an area stretching from Olancho to El Salvador.

At the time of conquest, the Lenca "proper" are thought to have been a relatively small group centered around the mountains near present-day Erandique. They had established villages but were essentially hunters and engaged in little agriculture. Loyalties existed only among those who spoke the same language, and tribes were constantly at war with their immediate neighbors.

Farther west, toward the Guatemalan border in the Copán and Chamelecón valleys and in the department of Ocotepeque, the Chortí Maya dominated. The Chortí were the immediate descendants of the Classic Maya who had built Copán several centuries earlier. Although they were a relatively sedentary agricultural society, their political organization did not extend much beyond a group of neighboring villages at the time of the Spanish conquest.

The first Spanish forays into western Honduras came from Guatemala, when in the mid-1520s an expedition led by Juan Pérez Dardón took control of the Río Copán region under orders from Pedro de Alvarado. By 1530, other expeditions from both the Honduran coast and from Guatemala converged on the mountainous region around Celaque, but they were soon faced with indigenous rebellions led by Lenca leaders Tapica and Etempica, the Chortí Maya leaders Mota and Copán Galel, and later the most famous of all, Lempira. Not until 1539 was the revolt extinguished and Spanish control over the region consolidated.

Part of the Higueras province, western

Honduras was extremely poor throughout the colonial period. The small mines of gold and silver found near Gracias were quickly spent, and treasure-seeking conquistadors headed for richer prospects in Peru and Mexico. After a few short years as the administrative center of Central America in the 1540s, western Honduras faded into a sparsely populated region, surviving on the meager income from cattle production and the tobacco industry.

To this day, the mountain highlands region of western Honduras is one of the poorest parts of the country, inhabited mainly by peasants, many of whom survive by subsistence farming supplemented by meager corn or coffee production. The banana plantations and—more recently—*maquila* factories around San Pedro Sula draw a steady stream of job seekers from western Honduras.

Copán Ruinas Town

For many visitors, Copán Ruinas is the first Honduran town they see after crossing over from Guatemala, and it's hard not to be charmed by the relaxed friendliness of the place. Any afternoon and evening in the square, one can watch schoolchildren playing, elders leisurely passing the time of day, and a young man plucking a tune on his guitar under the admiring gaze of his girl.

An attractive town with cobblestone streets, Copán Ruinas has an appealing locale amid the green hills of the Río Copán valley.

Copán Ruinas was originally a small village, an outlying settlement of the larger Santa Rita, before archaeology and tourism improved its fortunes and made it the largest town in the Valle de Copán. It has become the commercial center for the region, and these days is expanding to annex the neighboring town of Ostuman. Much of the agricultural land in the Valle de Copán was dedicated to tobacco since colonial times. For many years Copán tobacco was famed throughout the Americas and well known in Europe. In the 1960s, other tobacco strains were introduced to the valley, and pests brought in by the foreign varieties quickly wiped out the Copán plant. Tobacco is no longer grown in the region, but coffee plantations have taken up where tobacco left off, with shade-grown varieties becoming an important revenue source for the region.

The annual festival honoring the patron saint of Copán Ruinas, San José, takes place the week running up to March 19. Growing in reputation is the annual Conference on Honduras, a forum for national and international NGOs working in Honduras, in which a few hundred people descend onto the town and its hotels to exchange ideas and lessons learned. This takes place in early October—check www.projecthonduras.com for the exact date each year—and be sure to make hotel reservations in advance if your visit coincides.

Tourists can be spread out in other towns and cities across Honduras, but in Copán Ruinas they are concentrated into the small town with its big attractions, so you can expect to see plenty of other travelers around town. The plus to this is the plethora of restaurants and hotels to choose from, and a lively nightlife for a town its size.

A good website for information about the town and surrounding area is www.copan-honduras.org, with information about hotels, restaurants, and activities in the area. The national government has helped establish a website related to the 2012 celebrations, www.copan2012honduras.com, although as of early 2012 it was not yet fully functional.

COPÁN AND WESTERN HONDURAS

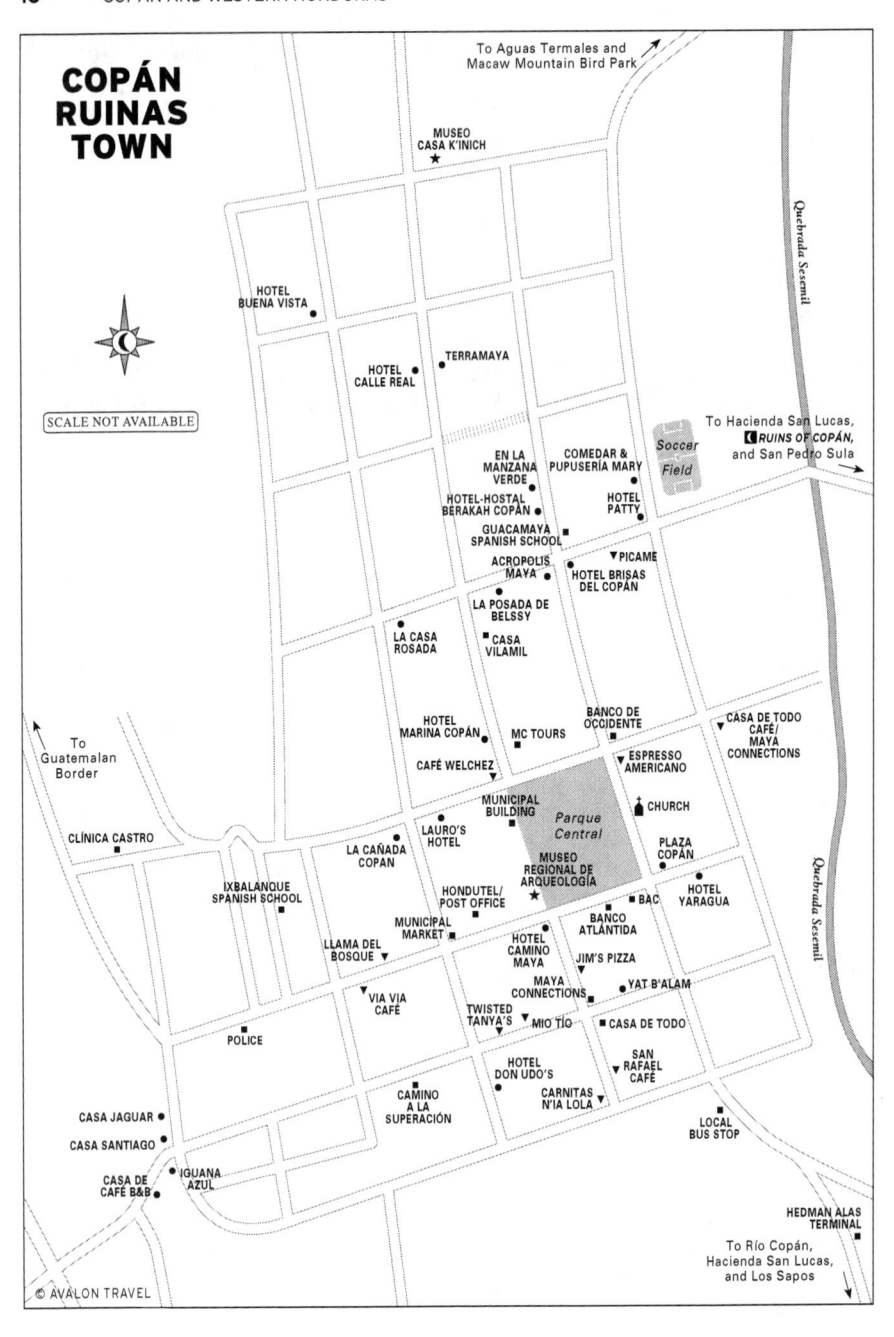

COPÁN RUINAS TOWN

the parque central at the town of Copán Ruinas

SIGHTS

The center of town in Copán Ruinas is, of course, the *parque central,* which was redone a few years back with a good dose of concrete. Although nothing on the level of the Museo de Escultura at the Mayan ruins, the small **Museo Regional de Arqueología** (tel. 504/2651-4437, 9 A.M.–5 P.M. daily, US$2.50 entrance) on the park is worth a visit to admire the complete tomb of a shaman, laid out in a case just as it was found at Las Sepulturas site, or the ceramic incense vessels covered with figures of Copán's rulers. Other items of interest include statuettes, jade sculptures, and a few of the famous obsidian flints with exquisitely carved Mayan faces. It was renovated just in time for the 2012 celebrations and is described by one of the ruins guides as home to "the bodies and the goodies"—that is, skeletons and artifacts.

On the north side of the park, housed in the old high school, is a new, permanent **photo exhibition** called "100 Years of Community, Copán 1912–2012" (2–5 P.M. daily, free admission). The exhibition is a gift to the people of Copán from the Peabody Museum at Harvard University and Harvard-affiliated, locally based archeologists William and Barbara Fash. It contains wonderful photos and interpretive material detailing the relationship between the village of Copán Ruinas and the archeological site during the past 100 years.

The **Museo Casa K'inich** (tel. 504/2651-4105, 8 A.M.–noon and 1–5 P.M. Tues.–Sun., adults US$1, children free), in the old *cuartel,* a barracks building atop a hill five blocks north of the square, is a small, interactive children's museum with displays of traditional musical instruments, Mayan numbers, and the Mayan ball game, geared roughly toward ages 5–9. Unfortunately, the low entry price seems to mean that there isn't much money left over for the maintenance of the exhibits, some of which are showing signs of wear and tear. Be sure to climb the ladders into the *cuartel* turrets for the expansive views over the town and the Río Copán valley.

The municipal market is located in a restored colonial-style building half a block east of the square; the piles of fresh fruits and vegetables always make for an interesting browse.

ENTERTAINMENT

Heading west past the Hotel Camino Maya, **Via Via Café** is a favored spot for the traveler crowd to have drinks in the evening, with happy hour 5–7 P.M., as well as events like movie night, salsa night (including an instructor) on Wednesday, and European dance music on the weekend, starting at 9:30 P.M. **Twisted Tanya's**, one block south of the municipal market, is a quieter spot, but it has draft beer from D&D Brewery at Lago de Yojoa on tap, and a large selection of fancy cocktails and shots. **Xibalba** at the Camino Maya hotel is another cozy spot to stop off for a drink. Our favorite beer in town is made by a German guy who asked to be left out of the guidebook, so just ask around for him if you're hankering for a good brew.

SHOPPING

As a major tourist destination, Copán Ruinas has its share of souvenir shops, many with Guatemalan and Salvadoran as well as Honduran crafts, including *junco* palm goods, leather, ceramics, jade and wood sculptures, and the ever-present T-shirts and coffee. The high-end shops at the **Yat B'alam** mini-shopping complex have unique pieces of Lencan pottery and stylish jewelry, as well as other goodies such as hand-carved candle holders and candles made by a women's cooperative.

On the corner of the same street is a branch of **Casa de Todo** (www.casadetodo.com), with goods from across Central America. Honduran handicrafts of note here include Mayan-design artwork on tree bark paper, baskets made of pine needles, candles made by a women's cooperative, and CDs by top local artists. Their other branch, a couple of blocks away, is a one-stop shop with Internet, laundry service, and a café. Another good multipurpose store is **Maya Connections** (7 A.M.–9 P.M. daily), with souvenirs, Internet, and laundry service.

Across from the Hotel Marina and just up the hill is another mini-shopping center, **Casa Villamil** (www.casavillamil.com), housing classy shops selling cigars, jade, silver jewelry, and handicrafts, as well as a coffee shop (with wireless Internet) and gourmet deli (6:30 A.M.–10 P.M. daily).

The hotel **Yat B'alam**, in the center of town, is also home to a mini-shopping center with three very nice handicraft shops, as well as a small café. Well-made Lencan pottery, corn husk dolls, and music CDs are just a few of the items available here.

A different kind of shop for finding a souvenir is **El Camino a la Superación** (www.elcaminoalasuperacion.com)—"the path to improvement"—an artists' cooperative working to develop the craft skills of its members while providing an outlet for their goods. Products can vary depending on what members are making, but during our visit there were colorful traditional Honduran dresses, stone sculptures, greeting cards, and hobo bags, as well as seed and bead jewelry made by another cooperative of Chortí Maya women.

If it's not raining, there are usually a few tables set up in the street perpendicular to the park, by the Hotel Camino Maya, although the selection of crafts here is rather uninspired.

ACCOMMODATIONS

Because Copán Ruinas is accustomed to tourists of all incomes, from backpackers to luxury travelers, hotels are available in all price and quality ranges. The majority are right in the center of town.

When arriving in town by bus, expect to be surrounded by a horde of young men who will offer to help find a room in any price range and will give you a ride there for free. We strongly urge you to avoid dealing with these men and boys, who get a commission for taking you to a less desirable hotel or on an overpriced horseback ride. Spring for a *mototaxi* into town (US$1) and get the room you really want, then arrange any tours through a reputable agency such as Basecamp or Yaragua, or through your hotel.

Although only a few hotels have swimming pools, the Clarion will let anyone use their pool if you have a meal there.

Under US$10

A few blocks west of the *parque* in a quiet neighborhood is an exceptionally good deal, the ◖**Iguana Azul** (tel. 504/2651-4620, www.iguanaazulcopan.com, US$7 dorm bed, US$13 s, US$16 d), with dormitory beds and small private rooms in a clean, airy lodge. In the back are the communal showers, with hot water, and an area to wash clothes. Lockers are available, as well as free purified water, and reservations are accepted. The lodge is run by the Honduran-American owners of the Casa del Café, next door.

Another excellent dorm-style hostel is ◖**En La Manzana Verde,** located a couple of blocks north of the park (tel. 504/2651-4652, www.lamanzanaverde.com, US$6 pp), with bunks and even a pair of double beds in a dorm-style setup. There is a *pila* for washing clothes, the bathrooms are cleaned six times a day(!), and guests have free use of the large, clean kitchen until 10 P.M. Reservations can be made by contacting Via Via Café. Both hostels have a wealth of tourist information.

Next door to En La Manzana Verde is **Hotel-Hostal Berakah Copán** (tel. 504/9951-4288, www.hotelberakah.wordpress.com, US$3 pp in a hammock on the porch, US$6 pp in dorm, US$16 s, US$17–20 d), a well-located hotel with simple, clean rooms. There are both ceiling fans and floor fans in the rooms to keep things cool, a bit of cooking equipment that guests can use, and everyone gets hot water showers and wireless Internet access.

US$10-25

The Belgian-run **Via Via Café** (tel. 504/2651-4695, www.viaviacafe.com, cafeviavia@gmail.com, US$12 s, US$16 d) has plain rooms at the back of the restaurant, perfect for crashing after an evening at the restaurant and bar. Wireless Internet is available, as well as yoga classes and massages. Another economical option is the **Hotel Calle Real** (tel. 504/2651-4230, hotelcallereal@yahoo.com, US$17.50 s, US$24 d), 2.5 blocks up a steep hill from the *parque*. The colonial-style hotel has a leafy sitting area, and its 22 rooms can fill up with groups, so it's best to call ahead.

A block away, **La Posada de Belssy** (tel. 504/2651-4680, laposadadebelssy@gmail.com, US$12 s, US$18 d) has similar rooms, as well as a rather dilapidated rooftop terrace with wading pool. The owner, Thelma, is reported to be very attentive with guests.

Another inexpensive and clean accommodation in town, near the highway bridge leaving town toward the ruins, is **Hotel Patty** (tel. 504/2651-4021, hotelpaty@yahoo.com, US$16 s, US$22 d), with sparse rooms with TVs, fans, and private bath.

US$25-50

A block north of the square is **Hotel Brisas del Copán** (tel. 504/2651-4118, US$21 s, US$37 d), with quiet, clean rooms with hot water, fans, and TVs. The owners live in the adjacent building, which is separated from the hotel by a small patio with chairs open to guests, and there is another terrace for guests as well—though the view is somewhat marred by the electrical wires and unkempt neighboring terraces. The same family also runs the **Acropolis Maya** (tel. 504/2651-4634, hotelacropolis@hotmail.com, US$45 s, US$50 d) across the street. Nice enough from the outside, the hotel's 10 rooms are a little dark and need updating (and an airing), but they are spacious and have air-conditioning and wireless Internet. Ask for a room on the second floor with a balcony.

Hotel Yaragua (tel. 504/2651-4050, www.yaragua.com, US$21 s, US$26 d, US$8 more for a/c), on the southeast corner of the square across from the Plaza Copán, has 24 dark rooms with fans, wireless Internet, and TVs around a small leafy courtyard. The upstairs rooms are nicer. Check the mattress, as some are mushy. **Lauro's Hotel** (tel. 504/2651-4068, www.laurohotel.com, US$25 s/d, US$15 more with a/c) is a comparable-quality choice, also close to the park. Ask for a room on the second floor, as those on the ground floor are fairly dark.

Hotel Buena Vista (tel. 504/2651-4464, www.buenavistacopan.com, US$40 s, US$47 d) is one of the best options in this price range, with 19 rooms set around a courtyard with a clean swimming pool and colonial furnishings. Its one disadvantage is that it is up three steep blocks from the main square, but it's an easy walk down, and *mototaxis* are happy enough to take you back up for just US$0.55 per person.

Another good addition to this price range is **Hotel Mary** (tel. 504/2651-4910, www.comedormary.com, US$25 s, US$41 d), located opposite the soccer field near the edge of town. Established by the owners of the restaurant of the same name (which is now located by the soccer field as well), the eight rooms are much like the meals at the restaurant—basic but done well, and clean. There is wireless Internet, and laundry service is available as well.

US$50-100

A unique setup five blocks southwest of downtown is ◖ **Casa de Café Bed and Breakfast** (tel. 504/2651-4620, www.casadecafecopan.com, US$52 s, US$64 d), run by an American-Honduran couple. Behind the lovely main house are several wood-paneled guest rooms, tastefully decorated and featuring elegant wooden writing desks. From the hammocks on the patio, you'll enjoy unmatched views over

lush gardens and a mountain view at Casa de Café Bed and Breakfast

the Río Copán valley below. This secluded place is perfect for relaxing and soaking in the area's vibes—but if you need further help relaxing, a stop at the tented massage pavilion is highly recommended. Room price includes a hearty, home-cooked breakfast, coffee and tea all day long, as well as any advice and assistance with logistics that you might need for planning your stay in Copán and throughout Honduras, from owners Howard and Angela. The hotel is about a five-minute walk from the *parque*.

At the southwest corner of the square is the pleasant **Hotel Camino Maya** (tel. 504/2651-4646, www.caminomayahotel.com, US$60 s, US$65 d), offering spacious and comfortable rooms with a TV, hairdryer, iron, and air-conditioning. There is wireless Internet throughout the hotel (there are also three computers in the lobby that guests can use), and rates include breakfast. There are larger rooms with small sitting areas, fridge, coffeemaker, safety deposit box, and DVD player for an additional US$15. Rooms have recently been renovated and have modern bedding and amenities along with colonial and Maya touches in the decor. The hotel also has a "recreation center" for the use of its guests, located at the edge of town—a short car ride or moderate walk away —with a swimming pool, children's play equipment, and hammocks.

Plaza Copán (tel. 504/3651-4508, www.hotelplazacopan.com, US$57 s, US$63 d), an imposing building on the *parque* next to the church, has 20 attractive rooms, all with tile floors, dark-wood furniture, air-conditioning, wireless Internet, and TVs, and a few with small balconies. The hotel also has a restaurant and a small pool.

Another elegant boutique hotel in the center of town is (**Yat B'alam** (tel. 504/2651-4338, www.yatbalam.com, US$75 s, US$87 d), which has just four rooms in a beautiful colonial-style building that is also home to three high-end gift shops and a café. All rooms have air-conditioning, wireless Internet, TVs and DVDs, and soundproofed windows, and the two rooms that face the street have small balconies as well. There is a small sitting area with views out to the hills, and the larger rooms can accommodate up to five people.

The rooms at **La Cañada Copan, Hotel y Suites** (tel. 504/2651-3416, www.vivecopan.com, US$70–93 s, US$81–104 d) are modern and spacious, if somewhat impersonal. Price varies according to size and amenities, and guests rave about the service. A swimming pool is said to be in the works.

The 16 guest rooms at **Hotel Don Udo's** (tel. 504/2651-4533, www.donudos.com, US$46–99 d) are each unique in layout and decor, and the price varies accordingly (suites and adjoining rooms are also available, at higher prices). The colonial-style building has a central grassy garden with the rooms (and hammocks) situated around it, each with air-conditioning and TV. Hotel facilities include a sauna, whirlpool tub, and a highly regarded restaurant/bar.

US$100 and Up

Romantic enough for a honeymoon or anniversary celebration is (**La Casa Rosada** (tel. 504/2651-4324, www.lacasarosada.com, US$145 s/d), catering to luxury-lovers with tasteful wood and rattan furnishings, and amenities such as showers that boast a steam function (complete with stools to sit on), as well as music speakers, a pillow menu, and local artwork. Rooms 3 and 5 have windows on the doors for peek-a-boo views of the hills when unshuttered. Rates include breakfast (usually served in the small courtyard) and a courtesy drink 6–7 P.M. each day. While there isn't a restaurant, the hotel can arrange for food to be brought in for lunch or dinner. One room on the ground floor has been accommodated for wheelchair access. Room 1 is slightly smaller and has the bathroom outside (although just two steps outside of the room, and behind a wall, so not within view of anyone else); it costs US$87 per night.

The owners of Casa de Café have also opened a six-room boutique hotel on the other side of town called ◖ **Terramaya** (tel. 504/2651-4623, www.terramayacopan.com, US$87–110 s, US$99–122 d). Rooms have exposed beam ceilings, handcrafted wood furniture, and Mayan motif artwork, as well as a small patio or balcony each. Breakfast is included in the rates and served on a back porch that overlooks a lovely garden (complete with massage pavilion, perfect after a day of strolling the ruins). Owners Howard and Angela make an effort to personally attend to each guest, and can help with advice or arrangements for tours and transportation.

The best-known hotel in downtown Copán Ruinas is **Hotel Marina Copán** (tel. 504/2651-4070, www.hotelmarinacopan.com, US$93 s, US$104 d). The 50 rooms in the attractive, colonial-style building feature dark-wood furniture and paneling, and a few have terraces and peaceful gardens out back—well worth requesting. Among the hotel amenities are a nice swimming pool, a sauna and gym, a bar, and a good restaurant (featuring live marimba music every Friday and Saturday night). Hotel service is very good, and some of the rooms have been recently remodeled.

Apartments

The owners of the Casa de Café B&B also have an apartment and a townhouse available for daily and longer-term rental (www.casajaguarcopan.com, www.casadedonsantiagocopan.com), with two bedrooms, fully equipped kitchen, a living area complete with library, cable TV, hammock, and maid service included. Both are spotless and tastefully decorated with wood furnishings and Mayan touches, and can sleep up to five guests if you don't mind having one person on the daybed in the living room. Casa Jaguar (US$90/night) has air-conditioning, while the Casa de Don Santiago (US$110/night) has ceiling fans in all rooms. Both rentals have a DVD player and selection of films and a CD player. The prices can be flexible depending on availability, and weekly and monthly rates are available as well (just $900/month for the Casa Jaguar).

Outside of Town

On the far side of the Río Copán from town, on a bluff just about opposite the ruins, is one of Honduras's best ecolodges. ◖ **Hacienda San Lucas** (tel. 504/2651-4495, www.haciendasanlucas.com, US$145 s/d) is a picturesque hacienda run by a charismatic owner, Flavia Cueva. Flavia is deeply committed to the nature, archaeology, and people of Copán, and uses the hacienda as a vehicle to preserve and support the community. Electricity came to the nearby village five years ago, and the painstakingly restored hacienda continues to make minimal use of it, relying instead on candles and solar electricity to light the eight guest rooms and dining area. The kitchen, reception, and outdoor dining patio are in the original main house, while the guest rooms are in three bungalows surrounded by lush vegetation. Rooms are simple but elegant, with cedar beds and locally made woven bedspreads. A hearty breakfast is included, but those in the know make sure to have at least one dinner on the property as well. The hacienda's local Chortí Maya staff hand-grind and pat out tortillas, to serve with gourmet versions of traditional chicken and fish dishes in fabulous five-course meals. The well-maintained trails in the surrounding hillsides are lovely for walking, and horseback rides can be arranged as well. A small Mayan archaeological site, Los Sapos, is on the hacienda property. Yoga and massages are also available (Hacienda San Lucas also offers a number of yoga retreats). Day use of the property is $2, or come to enjoy a late-afternoon cocktail on the grassy knoll overlooking a corner of the ruins, and stay for the sumptuous dinner (be sure to make a reservation, preferably at least 24 hours in advance, or they may not be able to accommodate).

An easy walk outside of Copán Ruinas, **Hacienda La Esperanza** (tel. 504/2651-4676, U.S. tel. 256/617-2468, www.haciendalaesperanza.org, US$87 s, US$99 d) is a homey hacienda-style bed-and-breakfast set up as a nonprofit for the Mayans of the area. Profits help support a small clinic and a local charity, Paramedics for Children, which provides school supplies as well as medical assistance.

Commandingly situated on a hillside above the highway at kilometer marker 164 (about three kilometers from Copán Ruinas) is the large, 80-room **Clarion Posada Real de Copán** (tel. 504/2651-4480, www.clarioncopan.com, US$115 s, US$121 d). The spacious rooms were recently renovated when the hotel joined the Clarion family, and the hotel decor has more of a colonial touch now. Of special note are the newly excavated ruins at the site El Rastrojón, adjacent to the hotel. The hotel is equipped with a sizable swimming pool and huge yard, two bars, a restaurant, and a conference room.

FOOD
Snacks, Light Meals, and Coffee

A couple of blocks off the main square, **San Rafael Café** (tel. 504/2651-4402, 8 A.M.–7 P.M. daily) is the place in town for a cup of coffee—or a latte or a Milky Way Cappuccino or any other kind of coffee drink you might be craving. Set in a small house with leafy garden seating, the spot is also a fromagerie, and those in the know order the Cheese Plate (US$10) off the restaurant's short menu of sandwiches and salads.

The **Casa de Todo** (tel. 504/2651-4189, www.casadetodo.com, 7 A.M.–8 P.M. daily) has a selection of wholesome snacks and light meals like granola with homemade yogurt and fruit, couscous salad, and pesto pasta (breakfasts US$3.70–5.75, other meals US$5–8), not to mention Internet, laundry services, tourist information, a craft store, and even a book exchange.

Café Welchez (7 A.M.–9:30 P.M. daily), right on the *parque*, has espresso drinks as well as sandwiches US$5–7), snacks, and fresh-baked cakes and pies. **B'alam Café** is another hotel coffee shop worth visiting, serving up coffee, sandwiches, bagels, and homemade desserts.

There is also a branch of **Espresso Americano** at the northeast corner of the square, and a branch of the chain **Super Jugos**, serving up fresh juices and smoothies, has opened near the south side of the square.

Honduran

The hands-down favorite spot in town is ◆ **Comedor & Pupusería Mary** (tel. 504/2651-4673, 7 A.M.–9 P.M. daily), recently relocated to a spot next to the town's soccer field, its wooden tables usually crowded with locals. Soups are popular with the regulars, and there are also well-prepared fish, beef, and chicken meals (US$5–8.50), *platos típicos* (US$2.50–5), and *licuados*, as well as their famous *pupusas* (US$0.60–1.15).

Budget-pinchers can eat at the stands located outside the market building in the afternoons and evenings daily.

Carnitas N'ia Lola (7 A.M.–10 P.M. daily), popular with the travelers, has tasty and filling nachos, quesadillas, huge *baleadas*, and, of course, the namesake *carnitas* (braised pulled pork, US$10), as well as other pricier cuts of meat (steaks run about US$15). An appetizer of **anafre**—bean dip with tortilla chips—is included with entrées, as well as a small dessert. If you're here for lunch, sit on the second floor for a good view of the hills. In the evening, the grill *(fragua)* is cranked up, and there is a happy hour for drinks and food from 6:30–8 P.M.

A step up in meat quality but a step down in atmosphere is **Mio Tío Parrillada Uruguaya**, grilling South American–style steaks for US$9–12. Chicken and pork are also on the menu, but there are no vegetarian options.

A block and a half west of the park, **Llama del Bosque** (tel. 504/2651-4431, 8:30 A.M.–9 P.M. daily) has been going strong for over 30 years, with an extensive menu including pastas (US$5–6), beef dishes (US$7.50), *plato típico* and breakfasts (US$3).

The ◀ **Hacienda San Lucas** (tel. 504/2651-4495, www.haciendasanlucas.com), in the hills across the river from town, offers an outstanding set five-course menu for US$28 per person. Made from local produce, the meal might include a fruit, green papaya and fresh cheese appetizer, cream of corn soup, tamales, chicken with the house *adobo* sauce or tilapia fish, and rum cake for dessert. Reservations are required for dinner, which is served daily at 7 P.M., although lighter lunches and breakfasts are available for drop-in visitors.

International

A Euro-style café run by Belgians, **Via Via Café** (tel. 504/2651-4652, 7 A.M.–10 P.M. daily) is one of several in a network of travelers' cafés around the world. They serve reasonably priced breakfasts and light meals, always with several vegetarian options, like veggie burgers and pasta, and a handful of daily specials, often based on Asian cuisine, such as Indonesian *nasi goreng* or pad thai. Breakfasts run US$2–3, while most lunch and dinner dishes are US$3–5. There are also a couple of inexpensive rooms for rent in the back, and the bar is frequently full of travelers in the evening.

Run by a British expat named Tanya, **Twisted Tanya's** (www.twistedtanya.com, 3–10 P.M. Mon.–Sat.), a block south of the municipal market, offers creatively prepared courses like curried chicken, fish in *loroco* sauce or beef ravioli for US$16 a plate, plus delicacies like brownie sundaes for dessert (you can order à la carte or pay US$22 for a three-course meal). If you don't mind eating early, three-course "backpacker's specials" are available 3–6 P.M. for just 6–10 bucks.

Don Udo's (at the hotel of the same name) is open daily for breakfast, lunch, and a romantic, candlelit dinner. During the day, snacks and lunch dishes such as croquet monsieur and mushroom ravioli are available (US$3.50–13.50), while dinner options include steak with your choice of sauce, salmon, and vegetarian ravioli (US$8–17).

Jim's Pizza (11 A.M.–9 P.M. daily), a block south of the *parque,* cooks up an acceptable, shareable pizza (US$8–10), as well as tasty burgers.

Pícame (tel. 504/2651-3953, 7 A.M.–10 P.M. daily), on the road heading out of town toward the ruins, is a good little joint with the best roast chicken in town, rice and veggie options, and a variety of sandwiches and burgers served on homemade buns (US$4–6.50). The owners have opened a tour and travel service on-site, so you can book that bus to Antigua at the same time that you grab a bite to eat.

INFORMATION AND SERVICES
Information

One helpful website is www.asociacioncopan.org.

MC Tours (tel. 504/2651-4154, www.mc-tours-honduras.com), across from the Hotel Marina Copán, **Copan Connections** (tel. 504/2651-4182, www.copanconnections.com), run by a British expat, and the tour office at **Pícame** can help arrange shuttle service to Antigua, local airline tickets, hotel reservations, and tours elsewhere in Honduras as well as around Copán.

Banks

Banco de Occidente, at the northwest corner of the square, changes dollars, quetzales, and travelers checks, and advances cash on Visa cards. It has an ATM, as do **Banco Atlántida** and **BAC Bamer,** both on the southern side of the square.

Communications and Laundry

Honducor (8 A.M.–noon and 1–5 P.M. Mon.–Fri., 8 A.M.–noon Sat.) is half a block west of the square, next door to **Hondutel** (7 A.M.–9 P.M. Mon.–Fri., 7 A.M.–noon and 2–5 P.M. Sat.–Sun.).

A better place for making calls would be one

of the many Internet cafés in town. **Inter@ Café** (8 A.M.–10 P.M. daily) is two doors from Via Via Café, **Maya Connections** (7 A.M.–9 P.M. daily) is a block south of the park, and the **Casa de Todo** is a block east of the park; all charge US$1 per hour. The latter two also offer laundry service. Casa de Todo charges US$5 for five pounds, and can have it ready as quickly as in three hours. Laundry dropped off early in the morning can be returned the same day, while afternoon deliveries are ready the next day.

Spanish School

For those who become hypnotized by the easy lifestyle of Copán Ruinas and want a reason to extend their stay, **Ixbalanque Spanish School** (tel./fax 504/2651-4432, www.ixbalanque.com) offers five days of one-on-one classes, a week of housing with a local family, meals, and even laundry service for just US$210. Classes are held in a restored colonial building, and the school offers tours, volunteer experiences, and even special language classes for kids ages 6 and up.

Another language school in Copán is **Guacamaya** (tel. 504/2651-4360, www.guacamaya.com), one block north of the *parque*. Five days of classes, four hours daily, plus a week's room and board with a local family costs US$225, while five days of classes-only costs US$140. Guacamaya also arranges volunteer vacations for US$135 per week, providing accommodations, meals, and Internet access.

Spanish classes and family stays in Copán are generally very good—the families tend to be more interested in interacting with foreigners than similar setups in Guatemala.

Emergencies and Immigration

The local **police** can be reached at tel. 504/2651-4060, although no local seems to have a very high regard for them. Your best bet in a medical emergency is the Red Cross (tel. 504/2651-4099), which can arrange **ambulance** service.

Clínica Castro (tel. 504/2651-4504, 8 A.M.–noon and 2–4:30 P.M. Mon.–Sat.) is run by a competent doctor who speaks English. His office is at the exit of town toward the butterfly farm.

All visa renewals need to be taken care of in Tegucigalpa.

GETTING THERE AND AWAY
To La Entrada, San Pedro Sula, and Santa Rosa de Copán

The best way to get to and from San Pedro is via two express services. The nicer **Hedman Alas** (tel. 504/2651-4037, www.hedmanalas.com) has a terminal a few blocks south of the *parque* outside of town. Hedman Alas has buses departing for San Pedro at 10:30 A.M. and 2:30 P.M. daily for US$21 in "Ejecutivo" class, while "Plus" service is US$26. Connections are available in San Pedro to any of Hedman Alas's other destinations (Tegucigalpa US$45 "Plus" service only; La Ceiba US$28 "Ejecutivo" or US$48 "Plus").

Locally owned **Casasola Express** (tel. 504/2651-4078) runs six buses daily for US$7 to San Pedro, the first at 5:35 A.M. and the last at 2:40 P.M. The ride lasts two hours and forty-five minutes, and connections to Tela (US$11), La Ceiba (US$12), and Trujillo, Omoa, Puerto Cortés, Tela, Tegucigalpa, and the San Pedro Sula Airport are possible. From San Pedro, the first bus of the day departs at 7 A.M. and the last at 2:40 P.M. Casasola's terminal is a block down the hill behind the church. You can also get off the bus at La Entrada (one hour, US$3.50), where you can catch other buses to Santa Rosa de Copán (one hour) or Gracias (two hours), leaving every hour or so between 4 A.M. and 5 P.M. from the bridge at the north end of town. Best to double-check all bus departure times, as they frequently change.

The 72-kilometer road between Copán Ruinas and La Entrada is paved, but fairly potted.

To the Guatemalan Border

The Copán Ruinas–El Florido border crossing, between Honduras and Guatemala, is the crossing most frequently used by Central American travelers. The road through Guatemala is paved and fairly secure, making this a better way (rather than via Nueva Ocotepeque) to get from Guatemala City to San Pedro.

Minibuses to El Florido, at the border, leave Copán Ruinas from the corner next to the market frequently and charge US$1.60 for the 20-minute, 12-kilometer trip. The last bus to the border leaves around 3 P.M. and returns around 4 P.M.

The border itself is in the middle of a field, with few services: a *pulpería* on the Honduran side, restrooms that cost three quetzales, and money changers offering bad rates. The border officials here are a fairly relaxed bunch, and crossing is not much of a hassle, although it takes longer now with the increased truck traffic. There is a US$3 charge for reentry into Honduras—we don't know why, but since an official receipt is provided, it seems legitimate. There are no charges at all by the Guatemalan office on exit or entry, so don't let them convince you otherwise. The border is supposedly open 6 A.M.–6 P.M. daily, but this seems to fluctuate. The best time to arrive is midmorning, well before lunch.

From El Florido, buses continue on the hour ride to Chiquimula, Guatemala, for US$2. You can catch buses from Chiquimula to Guatemala City for US$4—which unfortunately do not leave you near the buses that go to Antigua. If Antigua is your final destination, do yourself a favor and take a shuttle bus.

Direct Buses to Guatemala and Beyond

Hedman Alas (tel. 504/2651-4037, www.hedmanalas.com), with a terminal on the road south of town heading toward the river, has two direct, expensive, first-class buses daily to Guatemala City for US$58 (four hours) or Antigua, Guatemala, for US$63 (five hours). "Plus" service is US$65 to either destination. The 2:20 P.M. bus goes to both cities, while the 6:30 P.M. bus only goes as far as Guatemala City.

At US$20 the shuttle buses that run from Copán Ruinas to Antigua are a far better deal. You can book one through just about any hotel or travel agency in town, including Basecamp at Via Via Café. Connections can also be booked to Río Hondo or Guatemala City (US$20), Río Dulce, Puerto Barrios, or Cobán (US$29), or Tikal (US$39). Buses leave daily, at 6 A.M. and noon.

By Air

On February 4, 2012, **CM Airlines** (tel. 504/2445-0106, www.cmairlines.com) inaugurated a Saturday flight between Roatan and Copán Ruinas. To start the airlines was offering a day trip from Roatan for US$350 per person, including lunch and a tour of the ruins with a guide. For the flight only, the price is US$177 one way, US$354 round-trip (with the unfortunate schedule that you can either stay one day (so little time!) or one week (more time than most folks can spend). We hope there might be more frequent flights and connections to other cities in the future.

GETTING AROUND

Mototaxis are plentiful in Copán Ruinas, and a ride around town should cost US$0.50 per person. A *mototaxi* to the ruins normally costs US$0.75–1 per person, while to Macaw Mountain from town is typically US$1 per person. A ride out to Hacienda San Lucas is normally US$4.20 per group.

Tours

Basecamp (tel. 504/2651-4695, www.basecamphonduras.com), with its office at the Via Via Café and restaurant, organizes hiking trips, tours to coffee farms or thermal springs, horseback rides, and shuttle bus service to Guatemala and El Salvador. Staff are very knowledgeable on the area and happy to answer questions and point do-it-yourselfers in the right direction. A unique two-hour city walk of the "real" Copán is just US$10 and includes a US$4 donation to an education project; a three-hour horseback tour is US$15, and longer hikes run US$25–40. A two-hour "Copán Cultural Awakening" tour leaves daily from Via Via at 8 A.M. (US$10), walking the hills near Copán, including a visit to Los Sapos, and learning about everyday life of the Chortí Maya people. Foot and full-body massage services are also available (US$13–50).

Yaragua Tours (tel. 504/2651-4147, www.yaragua.com) also can organize a number of different excursions to destinations in the valley and surrounding hillsides, including horseback riding (US$20), sunrise and sunset hikes (US$15), visits to the hot springs (US$30), bicycle tours (US$20), and visits to nearby waterfalls (US$20–40). Yaragua can organize an excursion to a Chortí Maya community, where visitors have the chance to pat out tortillas and shape clay pottery (US$25 pp), or trips tubing on the Río Copán (US$15). Basecamp can also arrange all-day or overnight trips to the Finca El Cisne coffee plantation, while Yaragua coordinates half-day visits to other coffee farms.

With its office right at the ruins, the **Asociación de Guías Copán** (tel. 504/2651-4018, http://asociacionguiascopan.com) has the monopoly on tours at the park, but they also offer many more services, such as horseback rides to the Hacienda San Lucas and La Pintada (US$25 pp for 2–3 hours), guided tours to El Boquerón (US$50–60 per group) and other nearby sites of interest, and even guiding in places as far flung as La Ceiba and Guatemala. The guides are generally extremely knowledgeable, and many are multilingual (Spanish, English, French, Italian, and German are spoken). Two of their guides, Yobani Peraza (tel. 504/9992-8792, guiamaya@yahoo.com, speaks Spanish, English, and French) and Tito Ever Serrano (tel. 504/9967-6030, everserrano@yahoo.com, speaks Spanish and French), can also provide transportation service throughout Central America, in SUVs and vans.

Birders can contact **Alexander Alvarado** (tel. 504/3322-4082, birdinghonduras@gmail.com), a resident of Santa Rita de Copán and employee of the Macaw Mountain Bird Park, to organize bird-watching and hiking tours ranging from half a day to multiple days across Honduras.

NEAR COPÁN RUINAS TOWN

In addition to viewing the Mayan ruins, many hikes and excursions can be made in the hills and valleys around Copán Ruinas. Hotels can point you in the right direction if you want to wander the countryside, and local campesinos are helpful to visitors who lose their way. One can also stroll along the Río Copán in any direction from town and enjoy the rural beauty of the valley.

Guided hikes are also available, through tour operators like **Yaragua** and **Basecamp**, or with the **Asociación de Guías Copán** at the ruins.

Macaw Mountain Bird Park

A first-class nature-oriented destination in the hills outside of town is Macaw Mountain Bird Park (tel. 504/2651-4245, www.macawmountain.com, 9 A.M.–5 P.M. daily), a couple of kilometers outside of Copán on the road to the hot springs (take an inexpensive *mototaxi* or book through a tour agency to get transportation included). The beautifully designed bird park is filled with brilliantly colored macaws, toucans, and parrots from Honduras and elsewhere in Latin America. The park is a bird refuge, housing donated birds who have suffered as pets, and is spearheading an effort to bring scarlet macaws back to the Copán valley, releasing newborn macaws into the wild at the ruins of Copán. The wooden walkways, aviaries, and restaurant, built on four hectares of land in the heavily wooded Quebrada Sesemil valley, are lovely. Most birds are kept in aviaries, but in one area, visitors can hold the birds and take snapshots. There's a larger coffee plantation nearby with coffee roasters at work, and a coffee shop on-site, serving up Café Miramundo

Scarlet macaws perch on branches at the Macaw Mountain Bird Park.

coffee. The reserve costs US$10 (both dollars and lempiras accepted, children half-price); each ticket is good for three days of visiting. The ticket price also includes a guided tour, which is highly recommended to maximize your visit, so be sure to ask for it if it's not offered. There is an on-site restaurant, **Jungle Bistro,** owned by Tanya of Twisted Tanya's, that has a lovely riverside setting and offers breakfast (US$5.25–7.50) and lunch (US$8–16), albeit with steep prices. Note: The park will close an hour early if it doesn't have visitors, and it can also be difficult to get a guide in the last hour, so don't come too late.

Canopy Tour

Near the entrance to Hacienda San Lucas is **Los Sapos Canopy Tour** (tel. 504/9856-3758, US$35), a 14-stage zipline that takes adventurers across the Río Copán and ends at the southwest side of the Acropolis. To get there, take the road that passes the Hedman Alas terminal and heads up to the left.

Aguas Termales

A trip out to the *aguas termales* (hot springs), a 21-kilometer, forty-five-minute drive northwest of town on a rough dirt road leaving town at the corner by Hotel Patty, is a great way to spend a morning or an afternoon. The springs bubble out of a hillside just above a small river, out in a lovely area of Honduras countryside dotted with coffee plantations and small farms. If you don't have wheels, you can hop a minibus at the exit from town (take one heading to Agua Caliente), take a *mototaxi*, or book transportation through one of the tour agencies in town. If you travel by minibus, make sure you head back toward Copán Ruinas by midafternoon to ensure a ride. A small stand at the springs sells soft drinks, beers, and chips.

There are two large pools that are inexpensive to visit—and it shows. The water isn't that clean, nor that hot. Spend the US$10 for the private installations on the other side of the river run by Luna Jaguar (tel. 504/2651-4746), where small pools of varying temperatures have been tucked into the hillside. Amenities are limited (wear your swimsuit under your clothes or be prepared to change into it in the toilet stall), but the setting is lovely and the pools fairly well maintained. Massages are also available here, but better to save your money and spring for one of the better-quality massage services back in town.

◊ Coffee Plantations

Forty-five minutes north of Copán Ruinas is a century-old hacienda and coffee plantation, **Finca El Cisne** (tel. 504/2651-4695, www.fincaelcisne.com). The hacienda offers one- to four-day visits, in which travelers explore on horseback, learn about coffee and cardamom production, hike the surrounding primary forest, and relax in thermal baths as an experience in the farming life (tours in English or Spanish). Overnight visitors stay in an adobe guesthouse, lit by candlelight at night (although electricity is available for those who want or need it). Day visits cost US$70 per person; it's US$90 per person when combined with a night in the "Casa Castejón." It's possible to book your visit at Via Via Café in Copán Ruinas, stopping by the office between 8 A.M.–noon or 4–8 P.M.

About half an hour east of Copán Ruinas is **Finca Santa Isabel** (tel. 504/2651-4204, www.cafehonduras.com), the plantation and processing plant for Welchez coffee. Half-day tours are offered that include transportation from Copán Ruinas and a meal for US$30 per person. If you have your own wheels, you can come at any time, and the staff on-site will arrange the tour and meal for US$25. Numerous birds make their homes in the coffee trees, so keep your eyes peeled as you walk the trails.

Santa Rita and Vicinity

Eight kilometers northeast of Copán Ruinas, on the highway to La Entrada, is the cobblestone village of Santa Rita, which was originally the main Spanish town in the area. Formerly, the village was named Cashapa, which means "sweet tortilla" in Chortí Maya. If you need to stop to eat, there is a cowboy-style restaurant, **El Chaparral**. The last buses back to Copán Ruinas pass through at around 5:30 P.M.

On the far side of the Río Copán from Santa Rita, a rough dirt road winds up over the mountains to the southeast, ending up in **San Agustín,** where rides can be found to Dulce Nombre de Copán and on to Santa Rosa de Copán. The hike can be done in one day and passes along sections of the old *camino real* (royal road) and near the cloud forest of Monte Quetzal. You can hitch part of the way with passing pickup trucks.

El Jaral

On the highway toward San Pedro Sula, 15 kilometers from Copán Ruinas, is **Hacienda El Jaral** (tel. 504/2656-7091, www.hotelhaciendaeljaral.com, US$85 s, US$99 d, including breakfast), founded as a working ranch in 1870. Now run as a hotel by the great-grandson of the original owner, the hacienda is set around a large grassy field. Accommodations are in cozy cabins with stucco walls and wood furniture, each with hot water, ceiling fan and air-conditioning, TV, a mini-fridge, and a hammock on a small porch. There is a small swimming pool, a game room, a restaurant, and even a chapel, and weddings are occasionally held here.

A water park a few meters down the road is run by the same owners as the hotel. **Aqua Park** (9 A.M.–5 P.M. Tues.–Sun., US$4) has several pools and slides. Weekdays you're likely to have the place to yourself, which is a drag since they require 5 paid admissions to turn on the big slide and 20 admissions to turn them all on. On weekends all slides are on all day. While it's a relatively small water park, it's well maintained and can make for a fun day with the kids.

El Boquerón

Spelunkers shouldn't miss the El Boquerón cave, 20 kilometers northeast of Copán Ruinas on the highway to San Pedro Sula. To get there, follow the highway past Santa Rita up a hill called La Carichosa, then look for a dirt road turning left. Ask for El Boquerón (The Big Mouth), about an hour's walk from the highway turn. The Río Amarillo runs through the cave, so visits are best December–April, or you may be forced to go for a swim. Almost two kilometers long, it's filled with stalactites, stalagmites, and bats. Guides to the cave (recommended) can be easily found in Copán Ruinas. The Asociación de Guías Copán offers a day trip to the spectacular caves for about US$60 per person, which includes transportation and a meal.

The Ruins of Copán

Although not the largest Mayan city—at its height, a population of 24,000 lived in the surrounding region, as compared to more than 100,000 at Tikal—Copán was, as famed archaeologist Sylvanus Morley put it, "the Athens of the New World." For reasons that remain mysterious, Copán was the principal Mayan cultural center during the 400 years when the city was at the peak of its development, far ahead of other larger and more powerful Mayan cities in its development of sculpture, astronomy, and hieroglyphic writing.

HISTORY OF THE MAYAN CITY OF COPÁN
The Early Years

The rich bottomland in the Río Copán valley attracted farmers of unknown origin as early as 1000 B.C., but archaeological evidence indicates the Maya did not settle the area until about the time of Christ. Construction on the city is thought to have begun around A.D. 100, and the recorded history of the city does not begin until 426, when Copán's royal dynasty began. Some archaeologists believe the dynasty began when outsiders, probably either from the then-dominant Teotihuacán empire in Mexico or allies of theirs, conquered the city and took over administration of the valley.

Detailed information on Copán's earliest rulers is difficult to obtain, in part due to the ancient Mayan tradition of destroying monuments built by past rulers or building over temples erected in their honor. Not until 1989 were references to Copán's first ruler discovered, in a chamber nicknamed the Founder's Room buried deep under the Hieroglyphic Stairway. Apparently built by Copán's second ruler, nicknamed Mat Head for the odd headdress he is always depicted wearing, the room was dedicated in honor of his father, **Yax K'uk' Mo'**.

According to a stela found inside, Yax K'uk' Mo', the city's first ruler, took the throne in A.D. 426 and governed until A.D. 435. In an astounding 1993 archaeological find, the tomb of Yax K'uk' Mo' was discovered directly underneath the East Court of the Acropolis. Evidence indicates he was not a conquering warrior, but a powerful shaman who was revered by later rulers as semidivine.

Little solid information is available on the next seven members of the dynasty, apart from a few names and dates. Apparently ruling only a small, provincial settlement at that time, these leaders created few lasting monuments or hieroglyphics telling of their deeds. At that time, Copán's dynasty was thought to be consolidating control over its domain, as well as establishing trade links with other Mayan cities in Guatemala, non-Maya groups farther south and east in Honduras, and even civilizations as far off as Teotihuacán in Mexico, as evidenced by *teotihuacano*-style pottery in Copán tombs.

The Height of the Royal Dynasty

The period of greatest architectural construction, considered to be the height of Copán's dynasty, began on May 26, 553, with the accession of **Moon Jaguar** to the throne. Moon Jaguar, Copán's 10th leader, built the Rosalila Temple, which was discovered in 1989 buried under Structure 10L-16. A replica of the temple can now be seen in its full glory in the Museo de Escultura Maya.

After Moon Jaguar, a series of rulers of unusual longevity governed Copán, providing the stability and continuity necessary for the city to flourish. **Smoke Imix,** the city's 12th ruler, took the throne February 8, 628, and ruled for 68 years, leaving more inscribed monuments and temples than any other ruler. Frequently depicted in full battle regalia and

THE RUINS OF COPÁN

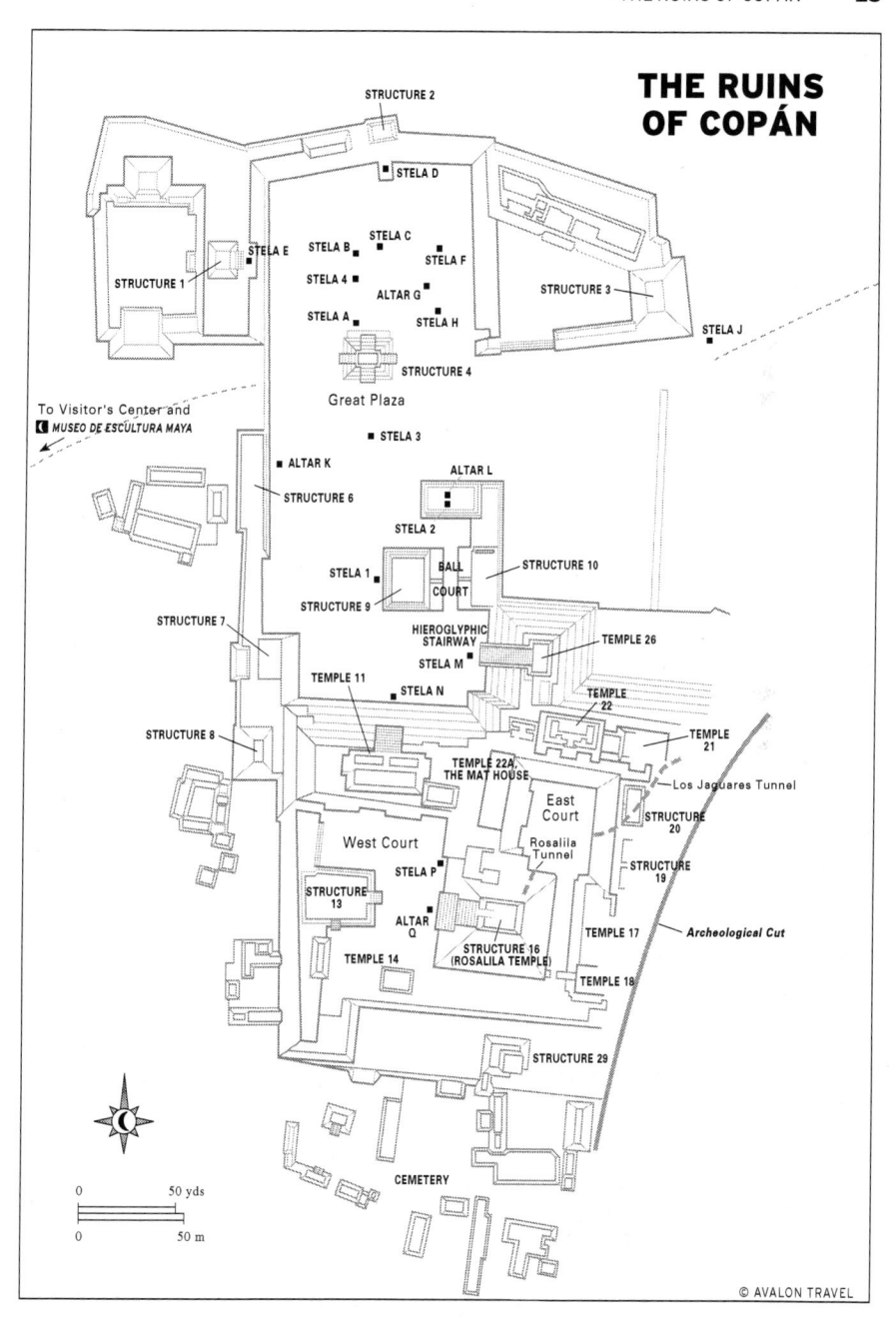

with representations of the jaguar god Tlaloc, Smoke Imix is thought to have been a great warrior. His successor, **18 Rabbit,** was also a prolific builder; he gave final form to the Great Plaza and the Ball Court. He also encouraged the development of sculpture, from low-relief to the nearly full-round style of later years. Despite these achievements, 18 Rabbit's reign ended in tragedy; he was captured in battle by the nearby city of Quirigua, formerly a vassal state of Copán, and beheaded on May 3, 738.

The Decline

Possibly because of the devastating blow of 18 Rabbit's death, the 14th ruler, **Smoke Monkey,** erected no stelae in his own honor and built only one temple during his 11-year rule. He apparently conducted the city's affairs in a council with nobles, demonstrating the weakness of the regime. In what archaeologists consider an attempt to regain the dynasty's former glory, Smoke Monkey's successor, **Smoke Shell,** dedicated the impressive Hieroglyphic Stairway. It is considered the longest hieroglyphic inscription known in the Americas, although recent studies have lowered the glyph count from 2,500 to 1,093. The glyphs narrate the glorious past of Copán, but the poor construction of the staircase itself reveals that Smoke Shell could not mimic the impressive work of his predecessors.

The final leader in Copán to complete his reign, **Yax Pac,** governed the city for 58 years. One of the most important monuments left by Yax Pac is the famous Altar Q, a square bench illustrating all 15 prior rulers of the dynasty around its sides, with the first, Yax K'uk' Mo', passing the baton of leadership to Yax Pac. Although he may not have known it when he commissioned it, Yax Pac left on the small stone altar a brief résumé of the city's entire history. Yax Pac built Copán's last temple, dated from A.D. 810.

A 17th leader, **U Cit Tok',** assumed the throne on February 10, 822. But for unknown reasons, his rule was never completed. The pathetic, half-completed Altar L, which he ordered built to commemorate his rule, suggests the dynasty ended with a single tragedy or defeat, rather than slowly fading from power.

The debate over the reason for the collapse of the Classic Maya kingdom has raged since serious archaeological work began at the end of the 19th century. The most accepted current explanation for Copán's collapse puts the blame on environmental factors and population growth. By the final decades of the 8th century, the city had grown to cover some of the best alluvial bottomland in the river valley; consequently, farmers were pushed farther up the hillsides, where land was not as productive. Recent investigations indicate that during this time the Río Copán valley experienced droughts, deforestation, massive soil erosion, and sudden floods during the rainy season. In addition, the Mayans followed slash-and-burn agricultural practices, which may have become unsustainable as their population grew. It's likely Copán simply outgrew its environment.

Although the city center was abandoned, evidence suggests the population in the region did not drop drastically until about 1200, when the region reverted to the small village groups found by the Spanish when they entered the valley in 1524.

◖ EXPLORING THE RUINS OF COPÁN

The ruins of Copán are about a kilometer east of Copán Ruinas on the road toward San Pedro Sula, set off the road in a six-hectare wooded archaeological park along the edge of the Río Copán. After buying your US$15 entrance ticket, walk up the path from the visitors center through tall trees to the entrance gate, where a guard will take your ticket. If you'd like to enter the **archaeological tunnels,** buy an additional ticket for US$15 (a high price for the experience, recommended for archaeology buffs only). (Tickets for the adjacent Museo de Escultura Maya are also sold at the visitors center, US$7 and highly recommended.)

Much of the original sculpture work at Copán has been removed from the grounds and replaced by exact duplicates. Although this is a bit disappointing for visitors, it is essential if the city's artistic legacy is not to be lost forever, worn away by the elements and thousands of curious hands. Most of the finest stelae and carvings can now be seen in the Museo de Escultura Maya.

Just before the place where the guards check your ticket is a kilometer-long nature trail with examples of ceiba, strangler fig, and other plants characteristic of the jungle that originally covered the Valle de Copán, worth taking a brief stroll along either before or after visiting the ruins.

The Acropolis

Past the gate, where colorful macaws hang out, the trail heading to the right brings visitors to the Acropolis, a massive architectural complex built over the course of the city's history and considered to be the central axis point of Copán, around which the rest of the city was focused. At the highest points, the structures stretch 30 meters above the Great Plaza (thus it was dubbed the Acropolis, or "high city," by archaeologists), and the many large trees still standing atop the huge structure only add to its imposing grandeur. The current Acropolis—perhaps only two-thirds as big as it was during the city's heyday—is formed by at least two million cubic meters of fill. Some of the most fascinating archaeological finds in recent years have come from digging under buildings in the Acropolis and finding earlier temples, which were carefully buried and built over.

A steep set of stairs leads up to the West Court, a small grassy plaza surrounded by temples to the underworld. The first stela you reach, Stela P, is said to be the oldest of Copán (although the one here is a replica; you'll have to visit the Museo de Escultura Maya to see the original). The figure in the stela is Humo Serpiente, or Smoke Snake (Butz′ Chan in Maya), the 11th ruler of Copán, with gods above him. At the base of Structure 16 on the edge of the West Court is a square sculpture known as **Altar Q.** Possibly the single most fascinating piece of art at Copán, it depicts 16 seated men, carved around the four sides of a square stone altar. For many years, following the theory of archaeologist Herbert Joseph Spinden, it was believed the altar illustrated a gathering of Mayan astronomers in the 6th century. However, following breakthroughs in deciphering Mayan hieroglyphics, archaeologists now know the altar is a history of the city's rulers. The 16 men are, in fact, all the rulers of the Copán dynasty, with the first ruler, Yax K'uk' Mo', shown passing the ruling baton—and the symbolic right to rule—on to the last, Yax Pac, who ordered the altar built in 776.

Between the West Court and the nearby East Court is **Structure 16,** a temple dedicated to war, death, and the veneration of past rulers. Heading around Structure 16 toward the East Court, one can look out to the right over the Cemetery, so called for the many bones found during excavations. Archaeologists later came to realize that the area was residential, where the royal elite lived. Homes were clustered around courtyards, and as per tradition, the deceased were buried next to their homes.

The **East Court** was Copán's original plaza. It is also known as the **Plaza de Jaguares,** for the two sculptures of dancing jaguars on the western side of the plaza, flanking a carving of K'inich Ahau, the sun god. Deep underneath the floor of the plaza, found by archaeologists in 1992 and 1993, are the tombs of Copán's founder, Yax K'uk' Mo', and his wife, who were both venerated by later generations as semidivine. The tombs were built at a time when none of the rest of the Acropolis existed, and are thought to have formed the axis for the rest of Copán's growth. Studies are still underway on the tomb discoveries, which for the moment remain out of public view.

Underneath Structure 16, in 1989, Honduran

REDISCOVERING COPÁN: THE FIRST ARCHAEOLOGISTS

Working our way through the thick woods, we came upon a square stone column, about fourteen feet high and three feet on each side, sculptured in very bold relief, and on all four of the sides, from the base to the top. The front was the figure of a man curiously and richly dressed, and the face, evidently a portrait, solemn, stern, and well fitted to excite terror. The back was of a different design, unlike anything we had ever seen before, and the sides were covered with hieroglyphics?.... The sight of this unexpected monument put at rest at once and forever, in our minds, all uncertainty in regard to the character of American antiquities, and gave us the assurance... that the people who once occupied the Continent of America were not savages.

John Lloyd Stephens,
Incidents of Travel in Central America,
Chiapas, and Yucatán, 1841

Copán became known to the wider world through the work of John Lloyd Stephens and Frederich Catherwood, two talented men who visited the ruins in 1839–and then, as the story goes, bought them for US$50 from a campesino. An American diplomat, adventurer, and author, Stephens had already published the famous travelogue *Incidents of Travel in Arabia Petrea* before he convinced U.S. president Martin Van Buren to send him on a diplomatic mission to Central America. Stephens was accompanied on the expedition by his friend Catherwood, an English architect and artist.

The pair spent several weeks at the ruins, clearing underbrush, taking measurements, and sketching buildings, sculptures, and hieroglyphics. After many more adventures and explorations in Guatemala and the Yucatán, Stephens and Catherwood returned to the United States and published *Incidents of Travel in Central America, Chiapas, and Yucatán*, which was an immediate success and went on to become one of the most widely read books of the time, going through 10 editions in three months. Stephens's detailed measurements and lively descriptions, accompanied by Catherwood's accurate and elegant drawings, captured the public's imagination.

Largely because of *Incidents of Travel*, British archaeologist Alfred P. Maudsley made his way to Copán in 1881. Although he stayed for only three days, Maudsley was entranced by the enigmatic and beautiful Mayan artwork. He returned four years later to begin a full-scale project of mapping, drawing, photography, excavation, and reconstruction that continued off and on until 1902. Maudsley's voluminous work on Copán and several other Mayan sites was compiled in the five-volume *Biología Centrali-Americana*, which was enhanced considerably by the superb drawings of Annie Hunter, still used in research today.

Maudsley was followed by a long line of Mayanist scholars, foremost among them Sylvanus Morley and J. Eric Thompson, who developed what has become known as the "traditional" model of Mayan civilization. Completely enamored with Mayan art and astronomical science, Morley and Thompson concluded that the Classic Maya were peace-loving philosophers living in something akin to a New World Athens, minus the warfare–an idea that held until the mid-1950s.

---

archaeologist Ricardo Agurcia found the most complete temple ever uncovered at Copán. It's called **Rosalila** ("rose-lilac") for its original paint, which can still be seen. Rosalila is considered the best-preserved temple anywhere in the Mayan zone. The temple was erected by Copán's 10th ruler, Moon Jaguar, in 571. The short tunnel accessing the front of Rosalila is open to the public for a US$15 fee, paid at the museum entrance. A full-scale replica of

The west court of the Acropolis

Rosalila is in the Museo de Escultura Maya, which gives a much better sense of the grandeur of the temple than what can be glimpsed through the two small windows in the tunnel.

The ticket price of the tunnel allows visitors to go inside a second, longer tunnel, which begins in the East Court and goes underneath Structure 20 to come out on the far northeast corner of the Acropolis. This tunnel has many more windows, which reveal sculptures of the temple beneath the temple. Both tunnels are well lit and have written descriptions in English and Spanish explaining aspects of Copán archaeology.

On the eastern side of the East Court, the Acropolis drops off in an abrupt cliff down to where the Río Copán ran for a time, before it was diverted to its current course in 1935. Since the river ran alongside the Acropolis, it ate away at the structure, leaving a cross section termed by Mayanist Sylvanus Morley, "the world's greatest archaeological cut."

Climbing up the northern side of the East Court brings visitors to **Temple 22,** a "Sacred Mountain," the site of important rituals and sacrifices in which the ruler participated. The skull-like stone carving on the side of the structure is of a macaw, the God of Brilliance.

Next to Temple 22 is a small, not visually arresting building called the **Mat House,** occupying a corner of the Acropolis near the top of the Hieroglyphic Stairway. It was erected in 746 by Smoke Monkey, not long after the shocking capture and decapitation of his predecessor, 18 Rabbit. Decorated with carvings of mats all around its walls, the Mat House was evidently some sort of communal government house; the mat has always symbolized a community council in Mayan tradition. Following 18 Rabbit's death, the Copán dynasty weakened so much that Smoke Monkey was forced to govern with a council of lords, who were commemorated on the building according to their neighborhood. The dancing jaguar carved onto the steps leading up to the Mat House is of Smoke Jaguar.

As you cross the small open area toward **Temple 11,** stop for the photo op looking out over the Ball Court. At Temple 11, take a look near the ground on the western side for the famous sculpture, **"Old Man's Head."** It is believed that there were originally four larger-than-life sculptures, to represent the "Pawahtuns," deities that the Maya believed to be the pillars that held up the four corners of the earth.

Temple 11 was built by Yax Pac, the last great king of Copán, and completed in A.D. 769. Experts believe that it symbolized a portal to the Otherworld, a foreshadowing of Copán's impending downfall.

The Great Plaza

After sneaking a peek of the Great Plaza through the trees, visitors head down a stairway that brings them to the extraordinary **Hieroglyphic Stairway,** the longest hieroglyphic inscription found anywhere in the

"Old Man's Head" is thought to be from a Pawahtun, one of the deities that the Maya believed held up the four corners of the earth.

of the stairway and thus read the long inscription left to us by Smoke Shell 1,250 years ago.

Underneath the Hieroglyphic Stairway, a tomb was discovered in 1989. Laden with painted pottery and jade sculptures, it is thought to have held a scribe, possibly one of the sons of Smoke Imix. In 1993, farther down below the stairway, archaeologists found a subtemple they dubbed **Papagayo,** erected by the second ruler of Copán, Mat Head. Deeper still, under Papagayo, a room was unearthed dedicated to the founder of Copán's ruling dynasty, Yax K'uk' Mo', dubbed the **Founder's Room.** Archaeologists believe the room was used as a place of reverence for Yax K'uk' Mo' for more than 300 years, possibly frequented by players from the adjacent ball court before or after their *pelota* matches.

Just north of the Hieroglyphic Stairway is the **Ball Court,** perhaps the best-recognized and most-often-photographed piece of architecture at Copán. (You may recognize it from the image on the one-lempira note in your wallet.) It is the third and final ball court erected on the site and was completed in 738. No exact information is available on how the game was played, but it is thought players bounced a hard rubber ball off the slanted walls of the court, keeping it in the air without using their hands. (A video, made by *National Geographic* of a re-creation of the ball game filmed in Mexico, is on continuous loop at the Casa K'inich.) Only the nobility of Copán were allowed to play (or watch), and it is said that if the game was political, the loser died, while if the game was religious, the winner died. Atop the slanted walls are three intricate macaw heads on each side—if the ball touched the ear of the macaw, the team earned a point—as well as small compartments, which the players may have used as dressing rooms.

The Ball Court leads out to the **Great Plaza.** In this expansive grassy area, which was graded and paved with white stucco during the heyday of the city, are many of Copán's most famous stelae—freestanding sculptures carved

Americas. It rises from the southeast corner of the plaza up the side of the Acropolis, and is now unfortunately covered with a roof to protect it from the elements. According to recent studies, the 72 steps contain more than 1,093 glyphs (which is far less than the 2,500 previously thought, but still a heck of a lot). It was built in 753 by Smoke Shell to recount the history of Copán's previous rulers. Since the city was declining in prestige at that point, the stairway was shoddily made compared to other structures, and it collapsed at some point before archaeologists began working at the ruins. In the 1940s, the stairs were assembled in the current, random order. It is thought that about 15 of the stairs, mainly on the lower section, are in their correct position. A group of archaeologists have been using computer analysis of photographs to try to re-create the correct order

DIGGING DEEPER

In the mid-1950s, as modern archaeologists investigated smaller pre-Classic sites and the residences of ordinary ancient Maya, a more complex, richer picture of Mayan society began to emerge. Not the peace-loving society that Morley and Thompson had once envisioned, it became clear that Mayan civilization had developed as so many others—amid warfare, trading, agricultural innovation, and exploitation of the lower classes.

Probably the most stunning breakthrough in understanding the Maya came in 1959 and 1960, when archaeologists Heinrich Berlin and Tatiana Proskouriakoff began deciphering Mayan hieroglyphics, a process that continues to this day. Archaeologists had long presumed that hieroglyphics were a form of writing, but they could do little more than guess at the meanings. It is now recognized that the glyphs are nothing less than a history of the cities where they are inscribed, recording in stone events such as battles and dynastic successions.

In 1975, the Peabody Museum of Harvard University, which sponsored Maudsley's initial investigations, began a second major project at Copán, a main component of which was to excavate the many layers of buildings buried underneath the Acropolis, in order to learn about the city's growth over time. Knowing that when successive Copán rulers erected new buildings, they generally carefully buried the previous structures intact, archaeologists undertook a project of tunneling under the Acropolis and back into Copán's history. One of the first results of this fascinating work was the 1989 discovery of the Rosalila Temple, with much of its brilliant original paint still visible, by Honduran archaeologist Ricardo Agurcia. The tunnel to Rosalila, now open to the public, offers a cramped view of the temple, while a full-scale replica of Rosalila is the centerpiece of the Museo de Escultura Maya. Tunneling farther under the East Court led archaeologists to a massive block of stone covered in glyphs, which appeared to be dedicated to the founder of Copán. Then, in 1993, several meters directly under the East Court, archaeologist Robert Sharer of the University of Pennsylvania and his team opened up what they and many other archaeologists believe is the tomb of Yax K'uk' Mo', the founder of the Copán dynasty. The tomb was built when the rest of the Acropolis did not exist, and it appears to form the axis for the construction of the rest of the city. Confirmation of the identity of the bones was provided by a jade pendant found near the skeleton's neck—identical to the one depicted on Yax K'uk' Mo' in the famed Altar Q. Medical tests determined the skeleton had a disfigured right forearm, which interestingly is hidden from view by a shield on Altar Q's portrait of Yax K'uk' Mo'. The University of Pennsylvania team, together with premier Copán experts William L. and Barbara Fash of Harvard University, continue to work on the ongoing excavations at Copán.

---

on all four sides with pictures of past rulers, gods, and hieroglyphics. Red paint, traces of which can be seen on **Stela C,** built in 730, is thought to have once covered all the stelae. The paint is a mix of mercury sulfate and resins from certain trees found in the valley. Most of the stelae in the Great Plaza were erected during the reign of Smoke Imix (628–695) and 18 Rabbit (695–738), at the zenith of the city's power and wealth.

All of the stelae are fascinating works of art, but one of particular interest is **Stela H** (built in 730), which appears to depict a woman wearing jewelry and a leopard skin under her dress. She may have been 18 Rabbit's wife.

Also worth noting is the round stone next to Stela 4, with a bowl-shaped indent carved into the top, from which curving indentations swirl down the sides. It is believed that human sacrifices were made upon this rock, the blood caught in the bowl-shaped indent, then running down the sides of the stone along the curved indentations, where it was either collected or spilled on the ground.

A wide path leads out of the plaza through a forested area, with many uncovered mounds

one of the intricately carved stelae for which Copán is renowned

among the trees—some 4,000 of them, according to one of the guides at the ruins—returning visitors to the entrance gate.

Las Sepulturas

Two kilometers up the highway toward San Pedro Sula from the main ruins is the residential area of Las Sepulturas. Ignored by early archaeologists, Las Sepulturas has, in recent years, provided valuable information about the day-to-day lives of Copán's ruling elite. The area received its macabre name ("The Tombs") from local campesinos, who farmed in the area and, in the course of their work, uncovered many tombs of nobles who were buried next to their houses, as was the Mayan custom.

Although these ruins are not as visually interesting to the casual tourist as the principal group, they are well worth a visit. The forested trails are always tranquil and uncrowded, and it is interesting to see the residential structures up close, which contain little more than bedrooms and tombs, as cooking was done in separate open-air common kitchens.

Most of the sculpture has been removed, but one remaining piece is the **Hieroglyphic Wall** on Structure 82, a group of 16 glyphs cut in 786, relating events from the reign of Yax Pac, Copán's last ruler. On the same structure is a portrait of **Puah Tun,** the patron of scribes, seated with a seashell ink holder in one hand and a writing tool in the other.

In **Plaza A** of Las Sepulturas, the tomb of a powerful shaman who lived around 450 was discovered; it can be seen in its entirety in the Museo Regional de Arqueología in Copán Ruinas. In this same area, traces of inhabitation dating from 1000 B.C., long predating the Copán dynasty, were found.

Las Sepulturas is connected to the principal group of ruins by an elevated road, called a *sacbé,* which runs through the woods. The road passes through private property, so visitors must go around by the highway. Be sure to bring your ticket from the main ruins, as you must show it to get into Las Sepulturas.

The men hanging out at the entrance offering guide service are highly knowledgeable, some having formerly worked as excavators, and their explanations help bring the ruins to life. Whether you use one of these guides or bring someone from the main site, you can expect to pay US$15 for the service.

Los Sapos

In the hills on the far side of the Río Copán, just opposite the ruins, is the small site of **Los Sapos** (The Toads). Formerly, this rock outcrop carved in the form of a frog must have been quite impressive, but the years have worn down the sculpture considerably. Right near the frog carving, and even harder to make out, is what might be the figure of a large woman with her legs spread, as if giving birth. Because of this second carving, archaeologists

THE RUINS OF COPÁN

> ## 2012: THE HYPE, THE REALITY
>
> Inspired by the celestial cycles that Mayan astronomers observed, the Maya created calendars of varying lengths, which interlocked to form a spiral (rather than linear) understanding of time. The Mayan calendar had 18 months, each lasting 20 days, for a total of 360 days. Mayan priests (who were the calendar-makers) understood, however, the 365-day year, and what followed was a five-day period where people stayed home praying for the 18-month cycle to begin again.
>
> These 18-month-plus-five-days cycles fit into a larger cycle of 52 years. One hundred of those cycles (5,125 years to be exact) complete an era that, according to the Mayan calendar, ends on December 21, 2012.
>
> But the end of the world? The Maya never predicted that. The end of an era. And the beginning of a new one—much like when one year ends and a new one begins.
>
> So go ahead and book those travel plans to Copán. No one there is expecting the world to end. But they sure are planning a good party to celebrate the end of an era.

believe the location was a birthing spot, where Mayan women would come to deliver children. Although the carvings are not dramatic, the hillside setting above the Río Copán valley, across from the main ruins site, is lovely and makes a good two- to three-hour trip on foot or horseback. To get there, leave town heading south and follow the main road over the Río Copán bridge. On the far side, turn left and follow the dirt road along the river's edge. A little farther on, the road forks—follow the right side uphill a couple hundred meters to **Hacienda San Lucas.** You can also hire a *mototaxi* to take you here from town for a couple of bucks. The ranch owners have built a small network of trails for visitors to wander along and admire the views, thick vegetation, and noisy bird life. Entrance is US$2. At the hacienda is a restaurant serving excellent traditional Honduran countryside food with products made by hand on the farm, like tasty fresh cheese, and a spectacular five-course dinner with revived Mayan recipes (reservations recommended). There are upscale guest rooms here too, if you'd like to stay for a night.

La Pintada

Higher up in the mountains beyond Los Sapos is another site, known as **La Pintada,** a single glyph-covered stela perched on the top of a mountain peak, still showing vestiges of its original red paint. The views out over the Río Copán valley and into the surrounding mountains are fantastic, particularly in the early morning. The site is near the village of the same name. Handicrafts are the specialty of the indigenous women here, who do backstrap weaving and make the corn husk dolls that are sold in town. By foot or horseback, La Pintada is about 2–3 hours from Copán Ruinas. Take the same road to Los Sapos, but stay left along the river instead of turning up to Rancho San Carlos. The road winds steadily up into the mountains, arriving at a gate. From here, it's a 25-minute walk to the hilltop stela. It's best to hire one of the many guides for a negotiable fee in Copán Ruinas to take you there either by foot or on horseback to ensure you don't take a wrong turn. The Asociación de Guías Copán also offers tours to the site, and Yaragua offers combination tours to La Pintada and Los Sapos.

Río Amarillo

Eighteen kilometers northeast of the Copán ruins, the Río Amarillo (yellow river) archaeological park has been excavated, opening just in time for the "end of the world" celebrations in Copán in 2012. The park spans roughly 30 acres and contains Mayan ruins within a forest preserve. The five stone structures, a central staircase,

VISITING THE RUINS: A LITTLE ADVICE

- The ruins are open 8 A.M.-4 P.M. every day. Entrance to the main park plus Las Sepulturas (one km away) is US$15, and the Museo de Escultura Maya (located right at the main ruins site) is another US$7 (all highly recommended). It's another US$15 to enter the tunnels—pretty pricey for the experience. It's very nice to get in right when the gates open. In the early morning hours, you'll be able to enjoy the ruins in relative solitude, and you'll have good low-angle light for photographs.

- Backpacks and oversized purses or bags are not allowed into the ruins site, but can be checked in with the ticket taker.

- When walking around the ruins, refrain from walking on stairways that have been roped off. Try not to lean on sculptures, stelae, or buildings—salts from your skin can corrode the stone, especially when multiplied by the 160,000 or so visitors who come to Copán each year.

- It should go without saying, but let it be said: It is illegal to remove any stones from the park.

- Two pamphlet-guides to the ruins are sold in the gift shop next to the ticket office as well as in many gift shops back in town: *History Carved in Stone,* by William Fash and Ricardo Agurcia Fasquelle, and *Copán, Legendario y Monumental,* by J. Adan Cueva. The former, written in English, has an excellent interpretation of the growth of the city and advances in archaeology, but does not discuss each monument individually. The latter, in English and Spanish, is weak on recent advances in archaeology, and although it does give descriptions of many major sites, they are often incomplete and not entirely useful. A recent addition to the literature on Copán is *The Copán Sculpture Museum: Ancient Maya Artistry in Stucco and Stone,* by Barbara Fash, is an indispensable handbook for those interested in the sculptures and carvings of Copán.

- Guides can be hired at the site for US$25 for a two-hour tour. Some of these local men have worked at the ruins for many years and have a positively encyclopedic knowledge about the archaeology of Copán—not just the names of buildings, but explanations on how archaeological views changed, when certain discoveries were made and why they were important, and all sorts of other details. In addition to providing information on the ruins themselves, guides often relate interesting local legends and tall tales about the area. Casual tourists may find their brains spinning with the endless stories of temples, rulers, and altars, but if you're really curious to learn more about Copán, you are definitely encouraged to hire a guide. They charge an extra US$10 to accompany you to the Museo de Escultura Maya, and US$15 for Las Sepulturas—both worthwhile expenses. If you're a solo traveler and looking to share the cost of the guide, try hanging out for a little while near the ticket booth, and ask those who have already hired a guide if they would like to share the guide and the cost.

- Although English-speaking guides are available, their language abilities vary. If your Spanish is nonexistent, check beforehand to make sure you and your guide can communicate well. You may want to consider contacting the **Asociación de Guías Copán** (tel. 504/2651-4018, guiascopan@yahoo.com) ahead of your visit to reserve a guide in English, particularly during high season (Holy Week, July, and August). Guides who speak French, Italian, and German are available as well.

- There are two gift shops on-site, a little restaurant, and an ATM. Craft vendors (with many Guatemalan as well as Honduran goods) line the fence just outside the ruins.

THE RUINS OF COPÁN **35**

a replica of the Rosalila temple, in the Museo de Escultura Maya

and a large mask are easily accessed along trails. According to local archaeologists, the structures are from the Late Classic period of the Mayan empire (roughly A.D. 600–900), with a ceremonial center built after the fall of 18 Rabbit.

Rastrojón

Another site unearthed in preparation for 2012, **Rastrojón** has been excavated under the direction of renowned Copán archaeologist William Fash, with the support of Harvard University. Located to the north of Copán Ruinas, vestiges include a temple built in honor of Smoke Jaguar, one of the great warriors of Copán, and a large quantity of mosaic sculpture.

Other Sites

On the far side of the Río Copán valley is **Stela 10,** another mountaintop stela, which lines up with La Pintada during the spring and fall equinoxes. Covered with glyphs, some of them badly eroded, the stela stands about 2.5 meters high. To get there, drive or walk 4.5 kilometers from Copán Ruinas on the road to Guatemala, and look for a broad, well-beaten trail heading uphill to the right, which leads to the stela in a 10-minute hike. This stela can be easily found without a guide. For those without a car, catch a ride to the trail turnoff with one of the frequent pickup trucks traveling to the Guatemalan border.

◖ MUSEO DE ESCULTURA MAYA

As of the summer of 1996, Copán has had a museum befitting the ruins' importance in the world of the ancient Maya. Designed by Honduran architect Angela Stassano, the museum is built into a hillside right at the main ruins site and illuminated by a massive, open-air skylight. Apart from the full-scale reconstruction of a buried temple, which is the centerpiece of the building, the museum contains some of the finest examples of Mayan sculpture ever found.

The museum's architecture was designed to depict different aspects of Mayan cosmology. The four sides of the building are aligned with the cardinal points of the compass, which were fundamental to the Maya, and also represent the four sides of a cornfield. The two-story design symbolizes the Mayan concept of a lower underworld and the aboveground reality. The first floor contains sculptures of skulls, bats, and other images of death and violence, while the upper floor displays facades from buildings and many of the original stelae commemorating Copán's leaders. The bat, or *zotz*, was the emblem of Copán, and is associated with the underworld, death, and sacrifice.

Visitors enter through the gaping jaws of a serpent, used by the Maya to communicate with their deceased ancestors, and a tunnel, similar to those used by archaeologists in uncovering the buried temples, tombs, and buildings at Copán, and meant to evoke a journey to the past. Dominating the center of the museum is a full-scale replica of the Rosalila Temple found under Structure 16 in 1989; the temple was built in 571 and painted a vibrant red—the color of luck, of blood, of sacrifice for the Maya. The bright colors may be a bit of a shock at first, but all Mayan buildings were once covered with plaster and brightly painted. It will certainly change your attitude toward the Mayan aesthetic—not one of somber elegance but a more exuberant, Technicolor style.

The museum houses many original sculptures that were taken from the adjacent ruins site in order to preserve them from the elements. It is here that visitors can truly appreciate the intricacy of the carvings—of woven mats, representing power; of cacao, the drink of kings; of toads, a symbol of fertility; of grotesque and monstrous gods, carved to inspire fear. One of particular note is Stela A, where the four main Mayan cities of the Classical period are represented in hieroglyphics—Tikal, Palenque, Copán, and Calakmul. There are also several buildings from Las Sepulturas site reconstructed inside the museum.

A visit to the Museo de Escultura Maya (Mayan Sculpture Museum, 8 A.M.–4 P.M. daily, US$7) is a must to admire the dazzling sculpture of Copán. Apart from displaying the originals of some of the best-known stelae and sculptures in the Mayan world, the museum contains many pieces never before seen by the public. These pieces give a full view of the prodigious abilities of the Mayan craftsmen. The informative signs are in English and Spanish. Take the time to read them all, or hire a guide (US$10) to draw out the highlights—it's a short course in Mayan history and archaeology.

La Entrada and the Ruins of El Puente

LA ENTRADA

Nothing more than a highway junction with a town built around it, La Entrada is worth stopping at only to transfer buses, or to visit the nearby ruins of El Puente, the second-most-developed Mayan site in Honduras after Copán.

Should it be necessary to spend the night in La Entrada, the three-story **Hotel San Carlos** (tel. 504/2661-2377, www.hotelelsancarlos.com, US$20–28 s, US$39–42 d), right at the highway junction, is the old standard, with comfortable rooms, a decent restaurant, and a swimming pool. Room prices depend on bed size (queen or king) and whether the room has air-conditioning or a fan. A newer and more promising option is the **Hotel Puente Maya** (tel. 504/2661-2311, www.hotelpuentemaya.com, US$30.50 s, US$50 d). The building is pseudo-colonial style, and the hotel and its 20 rooms are decorated with a Mayan motif. The hotel is located half a block from the store La Curacao.

While waiting for a bus to Copán (72 kilometers), Santa Rosa de Copán (44 kilometers), or San Pedro Sula (126 kilometers), fill up on *baleadas* and other cheap eats at El Triangulo store and lunch counter, next to the Texaco gas station. Buses to all these destinations frequently pass by, the last usually around 5 or 6 P.M.

There are branches of **Banco Atlántida** and **Banco de Occidente** in town, if you need to get cash.

EL PUENTE

Located north of the Río Florida valley on the banks of the Río Chinamito, two kilometers north of the Río Chamelecón junction, the modest Mayan ruins at El Puente (8 A.M.–4 P.M. daily, US$3) were first visited by an archaeologist in 1935, when Danish explorer Jens Yde drew a detailed map of the structures. El Puente then received little attention until 1984, when the Japanese Overseas International Cooperation Agency began work on the site in an effort to create a second archaeological attraction in Honduras (thus the anomalous exhibit on Japan at the visitors center). Of more than 600 sites identified in the La Venta and Florida valleys, only El Puente has been thoroughly excavated and studied. It is thought to have originally been an independent Mayan city-state at the far southeastern periphery of the Mayan zone, trading with the Maya of Guatemala and Copán and also with other Mesoamerican groups farther south and east. By the time of the Classic Maya, A.D. 550–800, El Puente had become a satellite of the opulent, powerful dynasty at Copán.

Because it does not have the incredible artwork of Copán, El Puente does not see even a fraction of the tourists of its more famous neighbor. As a result, it makes for a quiet, relaxing side trip on a journey between Copán and the north coast, if you've got a couple of hours to spare.

The 210 known structures at El Puente cover two square kilometers, but only the main group has been restored. Generally oriented east to west, the main group has five well-defined plazas and is dominated by **Structure 1,** an 11-meter pyramid with six platforms, thought to have been a funerary temple.

Other buildings of note include **Structure 10,** a long pyramid on the south side of Structure 1 that holds an ornate burial chamber, and **Structure 3,** a pyramid complex whose south staircase holds an example of an *alfarda,* an inclined plane of decorative stonework. Tunnels on the top of Structure 10 and on the side of Structure 3 allow visitors access into both of these buildings.

At the entrance to the site is a small museum with displays on the site itself and on Mayan culture in general, with descriptions in Spanish only.

From the museum, it's about a one-kilometer walk down a shady dirt road to the ruins, which are set amid grassy fields at the edge of a small river. Although the main buildings don't take long to admire, the location is a pleasant place to relax or have a picnic. A nature trail runs through a small wooded area, and you can also take a dip in the river to cool off.

El Puente is in the municipality of La Jigua, six kilometers from the La Entrada–Copán Ruinas highway on a newly paved road. The turnoff is at La Laguna, where you can catch a ride with a passing pickup truck to the ruins for US$1 or so. This road continues past El Puente to a lonesome stretch of the Guatemalan border. Traffic is fairly regular but not always frequent—better in the morning. A return ride can often be found with trucks carrying workers from the site back to La Entrada. A taxi from La Entrada costs US$12–15 round-trip, with a couple of hours at the ruins.

Santa Rosa de Copán

If you liken Tegucigalpa to Washington, D.C., for its politics, San Pedro Sula to New York for its business, and La Ceiba to Miami for the parties, then Santa Rosa de Copán would be the Berkeley of Honduras, a small liberal town that makes a pleasant stopping point for exploring the fascinating and beautiful western highlands, and for crossing between Honduras and El Salvador or Guatemala.

Santa Rosa de Copán sits on a hilltop with a commanding view over the surrounding mountainous countryside—including the country's highest peak, Cerro de las Minas in the Sierra de Celaque, to the east. Save for a local cigar factory, Santa Rosa doesn't boast any specific tourist sights in itself, but visitors frequently find themselves staying longer than they planned in this overgrown colonial town of 43,000 people. The climate is pleasantly cool, accommodations

SANTA ROSA DE COPÁN

[Map of Santa Rosa de Copán showing streets, hotels, restaurants, and landmarks including Hotel Casa Real, Hotel Castillo, Hotel Santa Eduviges, Migración, Parque Central, Catedral, Hotel Rosario, Cinema Don Quixote, Lavendería Wash and Dry, Hotel VIP Copán, Las Brasas, Post Office, Tourist Information, Hotel Elvir, Banco Fichosa, Banco Atlántida, Casa de la Cultura, Mass Bar, Banco Occidente, Hotel Antiguo Roble, Feria Agostina, Las Michoacanas, Hotel San Jorge, Alondra, Weekend's Pizza, among others. © Avalon Travel. Scale not available.]

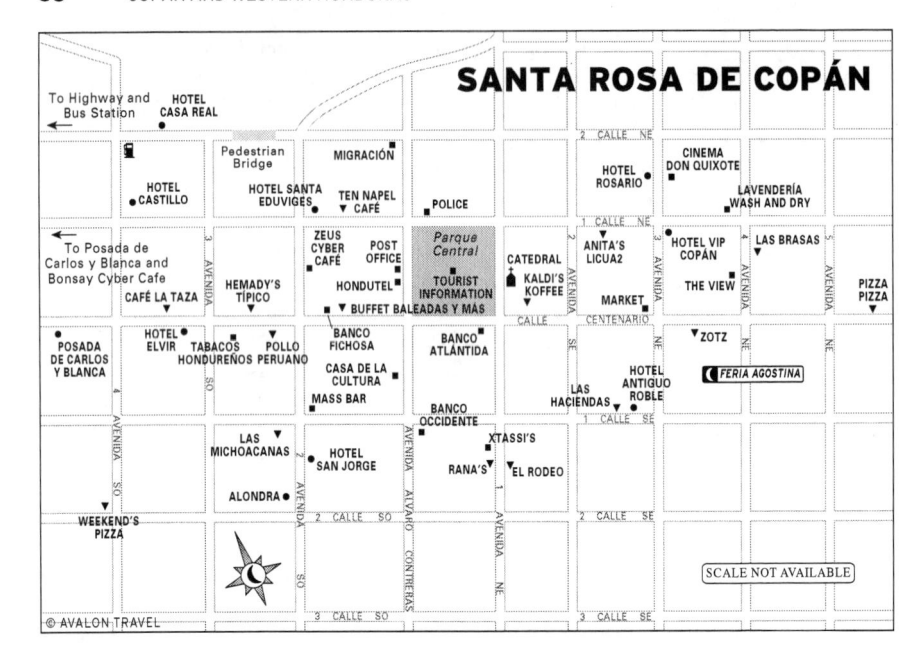

and food are inexpensive, and the residents are happy to see outsiders enjoying their town.

Although technically only the capital of the Copán department, Santa Rosa functions as the unofficial capital for all of the western highlands. Almost all commerce in the region passes through Santa Rosa, and campesinos from rural areas often wander the city's streets looking for merchandise or selling produce.

Santa Rosa takes pride in its colonial heritage, and the central section of the town is a protected area, with restrictions on building and renovations, to preserve the remaining colonial buildings.

History

During pre-Columbian times, the region around Santa Rosa was a transition zone between the Lenca tribes, centered farther east and south, and the Chortí Maya, who inhabited the hill country along the Guatemalan border. The remnants of indigenous villages have been discovered at several sites near Santa Rosa, such as El Pinal, Yarushin, and Zorosca.

Early in the colonial period, the Spaniards established a major settlement nearby at Gracias, but Santa Rosa itself was not founded until 1705. Juan García de la Candelaria, a captain of the Gracias town militia, applied for and was granted an *encomienda* in the name of Santa Rosa de los Llanos, also known as La Sábana. The site was strategically chosen on a hill above a fertile valley, along the royal road between Guatemala City and Gracias; the town quickly prospered as a transport way station and a cattle-ranching area.

A major boost in the nascent town's fortunes came in 1793, when the Spanish crown chose to move the Royal Tobacco Factory from Gracias to Santa Rosa, as the young town was nearer to the producing regions of the Valle de Copán. Santa Rosa grew steadily after this, with migrants coming from Guatemala and directly from Spain to establish their own small farms

the colonial church of Santa Rosa de Copán

and businesses. In the late colonial period and well into the 20th century, the tobacco industry based in Santa Rosa was by far the most important economic activity in western Honduras, and as a result the city quickly eclipsed Gracias as the most important urban center in the region.

Santa Rosa, along with Comayagua and Tegucigalpa, was deeply involved in the independence wars and the resulting strife between the different Central American republics. Honduran president José Trinidad Cabañas briefly made Santa Rosa the country's seat of government in 1853, when Honduras was under constant threat from Guatemala. In 1869, when the department of Copán was established, Santa Rosa was designated as its capital.

Orientation

Santa Rosa's downtown is a compact area of several blocks, but the town extends in all directions. The central market is east of the square, near the Ocotepeque highway, which continues down around the edge of town before looping northwest on its way to San Pedro Sula. The bus station is on the highway down the hill about one kilometer north of downtown. Taxis anywhere in Santa Rosa should cost US$0.75.

Addresses frequently refer to quadrants of the city: SO (*suroeste,* or southwest); SE (*sureste,* or southeast), NO (*noroeste,* or northwest), and NE (*noreste,* or northeast).

SIGHTS

In addition to the relaxed ambience, there's one actual attraction in Santa Rosa: the **Flor de Copán cigar factory** (tel. 504/2662-0185), formerly in the center of town but now in a larger location next to the bus station, a block off the main highway. Flor de Copán employs 240 workers rolling stogies for export as fast as they can, more than 30,000 cigars a day on average.

Entrance to the factory costs US$2, including tours in Spanish, which are given weekdays at 10 A.M. and 2 P.M. The original Flor de

Copán factory (now owned by Altadis USA), between the park and Hotel Elvir on Avenida Centenario, now serves as the company offices and store—no cigars can be purchased at the factory. Prices are generally about half of U.S. prices. The Santa Rosa mark is considered mild and smooth, while the Don Melo is considerably stronger, made with a Honduran wrapper, a Honduran-grown binder, and a blend of Honduran and Nicaraguan filler. The very strong and award-winning Flor de Copán line is actually now produced by Altadis's factory in Danlí. Both the cigar shop and the factory are closed on weekends.

Should you have a passion for coffee, you could also consider stopping by the **Beneficio Maya** (tel. 504/2662-1665, www.cafecopan.com), a coffee brokerage where coffee from the surrounding countryside is graded and processed for export. Tours are informal and free, but only offered during coffee season (November–February). The building is one kilometer west of the bus terminal.

The simple, whitewashed *catedral* on the square was finished in 1803. Under the watch of Bishop Monsignor Ángel María Navarro, it was reconstructed in 1948 with a larger altar and other improvements. The interior isn't fancy, but it is attractive with bronze chandeliers, carved wooden pews, and mosaic floors.

In the middle of the square is a two-story kiosk that houses the tourist information booth (tel. 504/2662-2234, turismosrc@yahoo.com, 7 A.M.–6 P.M. Mon.–Sat., 10 A.M.–6 P.M. Sun.), although limited English is spoken by the staff, and they don't offer much more than information on hotels. They do have a couple of computers and Internet access for US$0.75 per hour and sell **Copan Dry,** a locally made fruit soft drink. The office can arrange tours of the city center and a local organic farm, including lunch, with one day's notice (Spanish only). Some information about Santa Rosa in Spanish is also available on the website www.todocopan.com; another helpful site is http://srcopan.vze.com, created and managed by local resident Warren Post.

A block south of the square is the **Casa de la Cultura,** which sells books and artwork and has some information on the city and surrounding region.

Several high points near Santa Rosa offer fine views over the town and surrounding countryside on a clear day. One close point is **El Cerrito,** reached by following Avenida Centenario west until the cobblestones end, then following the stairs up to the hilltop. Farther off is the **Hondutel tower,** about a 45-minute walk from town, starting south along 3 Avenida SO.

ENTERTAINMENT
Festivals and Events

Semana Santa, or Easter Week, is quite a spectacle in Santa Rosa, with elaborate parades throughout the week. Locals create beautiful carpets of colored sawdust and flowers on the streets for the processions to walk on. The culminating parade is the Via Crucis on Friday morning, with "Jesus" carrying his cross through town in a solemn procession.

Another great time to visit is during one of the thrice-annual **Feria de los Llanos.** This artisanal fair with music and cultural performances is held August 25–30, the second week of April, and the second week of December.

◖ FERIA AGOSTINA

A quiet colonial town most of the year, Santa Rosa bursts to life during August, when *copanecos* celebrate their patron saint, the Virgin of Santa Rosa de Lima, with music, food, sporting competitions, and other events. Highlights include the artisanal fair, called **Feria de los Llanos,** held the last week of August, which includes music and cultural performances; the **Noche de Fumadores** (on the third Friday of August), an evening dedicated to fine cigars; and the **Tarde con Aroma a Café,** an afternoon tasting locally grown coffee.

HOLY WEEK IN SANTA ROSA DE COPÁN

While Comayagua is famed for its Holy Week celebrations, *Copanecos* put on impressive processions throughout the week to reenact the events of Jesus's final week, his death, and resurrection. The town typically posts a schedule of services and processions on the door of the cathedral at the town square.

- **Palm Sunday:** There are several services around town, but the 8 A.M. mass at the **Iglesia de San Martín** is the one to attend, as it's followed by a procession to the cathedral. Evening masses are then held at the cathedral Monday, Tuesday, and Holy Wednesday, at 5 P.M.
- **Maundy Thursday:** At 7 P.M. there is a special Eucharist mass in remembrance of the Last Supper, followed by a washing of feet and a procession. The Procesión de Prendimiento, to remember Jesus's capture by the Romans and incarceration, begins at 10 P.M. at the **Iglesia de las Misericordias** and ends at the cathedral.
- **Good Friday:** Flower and sawdust carpets are laid on the street for the Via Crucis, known in English as the Stations of the Cross, which remembers Jesus's journey to Golgotha with the cross on his shoulders. The procession begins at 8 A.M. at the cathedral and follows a two-kilometer route around town. Arrive early to view the carpets before they are trampled by the processioners. A reenactment of the crucifixion is held at noon. At 3 P.M. there is another procession, in remembrance of Jesus's burial. At 9 P.M. there is a procession in honor of the "Virgin of Loneliness," an all-woman procession illuminated by candlelight.
- **Holy Saturday:** An Easter Vigil service is held at 10 P.M.
- **Easter Sunday:** Those late to bed or very early to rise have the chance to witness the **Carreritas de San Juan** at 4 A.M., when a statue of Saint John is raced from the cathedral to the **Iglesia de San Antonio,** in representation of John racing to tell the Virgin Mary that Jesus has been resurrected. An hour later the final procession of the week departs from the Iglesia de San Antonio, bearing Jesus back to the cathedral, and is followed by Easter Mass. There are several more services during the day for those who can't get out of bed quite that early.

Other events during the month include **Juegos Florales,** a literary competition hosted by the Casa de la Cultura, and the **Feria de Ganaderos,** a cattle expo held in the AGAC field in the Colonia Miraflores. Goods ranging from hand crafted saddles to handicrafts and cheap toys are sold, and those looking to spice up their visit can try their luck at the mechanical bull or on the dance floor.

Bars

One good option is to go to the bar at **El Rodeo** restaurant for a few drinks, particularly when there is live music (Thurs.–Sat.). They have a full menu as well. Just across the street is **Ranas** (11 A.M.–10 P.M. Mon.–Sat.), with a little less atmosphere, but a little more nightlife: karaoke Monday–Wednesday, live "music from yesterday" on Thursday, and live salsa on Friday and Saturday. The menu is short here—sandwiches, burgers, nachos, tacos—just a few things to go with your drinks. A couple of doors down is **Xtassi's Discotec,** if you want to dance and the music at El Rodeo or Ranas doesn't suit your taste.

Zotz, two blocks from the *parque,* (noon until late Wed.–Sat.) has the aura of a restaurant like Hard Rock Café, with a convivial atmosphere and walls packed with memorabilia and antique pictures of Honduras. They offer a full menu as well (even with unusual dishes such as fish in vermouth sauce).

The place to wear high heels (if you're a

woman that is) and have a fancy cocktail is **The View,** three blocks east from the park. Another alternative to the usual bar is **Mass Bar,** an open-air spot that is combining "fitness, *fútbol,* bar."

Movies

Cinema Don Quixote (Plaza Saavedra, 3 Av. NE, across from Hotel Rosario) shows late-release movies from the United States every day at 7 P.M. for US$2. Tuesday is two-for-one, and the movies change weekly on Friday.

SHOPPING

Although Santa Rosa doesn't see all that many tourists, it has several unique locally made products that can make good souvenirs. Coffee and cigars are the obvious choices: There is a *tienda de puros,* or cigar shop, at **Tabacos Hondureños** (8 A.M.–noon and 1:30–5 P.M. Mon.–Fri., 8 A.M.–noon Sat.) along Calle Centenario. Three Flor de Copán cigars in a paper box sell for around US$9, while five Don Melo cigars in a wooden box are around US$17. (According to the sales clerk, the quality of the two brands is the same; the difference in price is because of the difference in packaging.)

Coffee is just one of the local specialties for imbibing. **Timoshenko** is a local company making both coffee liqueur and a fruit liqueur, found in a few local stores (along with other brands of local coffee liqueur). If you prefer your drinks soft, **Copan Dry** is a local company selling brightly colored sodas in six fruit flavors (plus cream soda). A little hard to pack as a souvenir, but worth trying while in town!

For more typical souvenirs, including a bit of pottery, try **Artesanías Rossy,** on the street behind the church.

ACCOMMODATIONS

There are several budget and midrange options for accommodations in Santa Rosa. Most hotels are within three blocks of the park.

Under US$25

The best budget option in town, **Hotel Santa Eduviges** (tel. 504/2662-0380, US$13 s, US$21 d), two blocks from the park, has 17 simple rooms with private bathrooms, TVs, fans, and hot water. The hotel is well maintained and rooms are clean and pleasant, all in all a good value.

If the Eduviges is booked up, an acceptable alternative is **Hotel Castillo** (tel. 504/2662-0368, US$13 s, US$18.50 d), one block away. The family-owned hotel is basic, but staff is friendly and rooms are clean.

Although you get what you pay for, if you're running low on cash, **Hotel Rosario** (tel. 504/2662-0211, US$8 pp shared bath or US$11 pp private bath), half a block north of Hotel Copán, is... well, cheap. Cold water only, not all toilets have seats, and the bulbs hang bare, but fresh air blows through the hallway and the older couple who run the hotel are pleasant.

US$25-50

Located on Avenida 2 SO, **Hotel San Jorge** (tel. 504/2662-2521, www.hotelsanjorge.4t.com, US$21 s, US$32 d, a/c available for US$5 more) is popular with mission groups, who rave about the friendly and helpful staff. Rooms are rather bare with ugly Formica flooring, but very spacious, and there is parking, wireless Internet, and a *pila* on the roof where you can either wash your clothes or pay for them to do it. The hotel has a full-service restaurant as well.

Just across the street is **Alondra** (tel. 504/2662-1194, US$17–25 s, US$23–34 d), another family-owned hotel in a stone building. Room prices vary along with their quality—the cheapest (on the ground floor) smell of mildew in the rooms and of stinky pipes in the bathrooms. The second and third floor rooms are much newer and nicer, although a bit pricey for what they are. Wireless Internet is available in all the rooms.

A newer hotel with a charming old colonial

style is the **Hotel Antiguo Roble** (tel. 504/2662-0472, hotelantiguoroble@hotmail.es, US$29 s, US$41 d), half a block east of BAMER bank. The hotel has clean rooms, wireless Internet in the lobby, and a coffee shop. Breakfast is included in the rates, which are about US$3 cheaper on weekends and US$5 more with air-conditioning. The hotel is popular with mission groups.

Another good option in this price range is the **Posada de Carlos y Blanca Bed and Breakfast** (tel. 504/2662-4020, www.posadacarlosyblanca.com, US$23 s, US$35 d). The house has five clean, cute, and colorful rooms, a nice living room where guests can relax, and wireless Internet. One of the rooms, with its own entrance from the front yard, has a tiny second room, good for families who want to tuck the children away and not have to go to sleep themselves (US$35).

A step up in amenities (but perhaps a step down in charm) is **Hotel Casa Real** (tel. 504/2662-0802, www.hotelcasarealsrc.com, US$35 s, US$38 d with fan, around US$10 more for a/c), four blocks northwest of the *parquet*. The hotel has all the amenities—wireless Internet throughout the hotel, a nice, clean swimming pool, and a restaurant open until 10 P.M.—but lacks a little on personality. The 52 modern rooms have big flat-screen TVs and little desks, but are all on the small side, and the bedding has a dated look. Business travelers seem to be the hotel's primary clientele.

Hotel VIP Copán (tel. 504/2662-1576, US$23 s, US$37 d), two blocks east of the church, has smallish rooms, a sometimes-clean swimming pool, a restaurant, and parking. Rooms with air-conditioning are larger and nicer, but cost about US$10 more.

For travelers getting in late and leaving early, **Hotel Posada Maya** (tel. 504/2662-4848, US$26 s, US$37 d), across from the bus station on the highway below town, is a convenient choice. Rooms are modern and fairly nondescript, but do have wireless Internet.

US$50 and Up

The best hotel in town is **Hotel Elvir** (tel. 504/2662-0805, www.hotelelvir.com, US$55 s, US$69 d), three blocks west of the park on Calle Centenario. The hotel has a colonial feel with a small interior garden, there is wireless Internet throughout the hotel, and the large rooms on the second floor have been recently remodeled, with flat-screen TVs put in. About 10–20 percent is taken off the prices above for the older rooms on the first floor. The staff is helpful, and the cafeteria serves tasty and reasonably priced food. Max Elvir, an enthusiastic promoter of small-scale tourism in the area, runs **Lenca Travel** (tel. 504/9997-5340, lencatours@gmail.com) out of the hotel, offering tours of surrounding villages and natural areas, including Celaque, Monte Quetzal, Belén Gualcho, San Manuel Colohete, and any other place you might want to visit. Rates depend on how many people want to go, and Max—who speaks English—is an excellent and affable guide. If you have your own wheels, Max charges US$75 per day for guiding only.

FOOD
Snacks and Coffee

Ten Napel Café, on 1 Calle NE, next to Banco Atlántida, has great wooden decor, free wireless Internet, and an outdoor garden, and serves posh coffee and snacks, including bagels.

Café La Taza (tel. 504/2667-7161, 9 A.M.–7 P.M. Mon.–Sat.) is considered by many locals to have the best coffee in Santa Rosa. It may also be the priciest (US$2 for a *macchiato*!), but it sure is good, strong coffee. The little café near Hotel Elvir has a nice atmosphere to hang out in and plenty of treats (cinnamon rolls, croissants, carrot cake, cheesecake) to go with your coffee. *Licuados* are served here too.

Giving La Taza a run for its money is **Kaldi's Koffee** (10:30 A.M.–7 P.M. Mon.–Sat.), an artsy coffee shop on the *peatonal* next to the church, with a couple of outdoor tables. In addition to the usual coffee drinks, Kaldi's sells coffee by the pound, including a number of exotic international coffees that range from US$5–13 (exorbitant prices by Honduran standards). They serve a few sweet pastries to accompany their brews.

Although they are Mexican-style, the *paletas*, or popsicles, at **Las Michoacanas** are 100 percent Honduran, made by a company based in Choluteca, in southern Honduras. Fruit-based flavors include dragon fruit, pineapple with chile, and passion fruit, while the milk-based popsicles include flavors such as cappuccino, lemon pie, and *arroz con leche*. The perfect way to cool down on one of Santa Rosa's sunny days.

Specializing in fruit smoothies is **Anita's Licua2** (pronounced *licuados*), along 1 Calle NE.

Honduran

For breakfast, there's a cluster of inexpensive places just west of Hotel Elvir, and also along 1 Calle NE between 2 and 3 Avenidas.

Pollo Peruano, on Calle Centenario a block west of the park, serves good chicken and fries for US$4.

Buffet Baleadas y Más has the best *baleadas* in town (US$0.60 for a *simple*, US$0.75 with egg or avocado), as well as a *plato del día*, usually chicken or beef.

Hemady's Típico (8 A.M.–10 P.M. daily), 1.5 blocks west of the park on Centenario, is tucked inside the former home of Dr. Juan Ángel Arias Bográn, president of Honduras in 1903. It's a simple restaurant with good renditions of Honduran classics for US$2–6, and also has specialties that can be hard to find elsewhere, such as *atol chuco*, a drink made with beans, corn, and food coloring; *ticucos*, a kind of round tamal, wrapped in corn husks; *atol de piña*, a pineapple drink thickened with cornstarch; and *pupusas*, a type of tortilla stuffed with cheese, beans, pork, or some combination thereof.

A step up is **Las Haciendas** (US$3–7 per entrée). One good, low-price deal is the large sandwich for US$2. They are open until late (midnight-ish) most nights, and even later (3 A.M.) on the second and fourth Saturdays of the month, when they host live music.

A block and a half south of the park is **El Rodeo** (tel. 504/2662-0697, 10 A.M. onwards, closed Sunday) with a good *plato típico*, nachos, hamburgers (all US$5), and inexpensive drinks. Pricier dishes like *pinchos* (meat on a stick) and steaks are on the menu as well (US$7–10). They have live music Thursday–Saturday, when they stay open until 3 A.M. Owned by the mayor, this is one of the places the local intelligentsia and cowboys alike come to hang out.

If you're hungry while waiting for the bus, the *comedor* at the terminal serves fried chicken, and the **JM** buffet restaurant right nearby has a hearty all-you-can-eat buffet for US$5 per person.

International

Set in a restored colonial home, the American-owned **Pizza Pizza** (tel. 504/2662-1104, http://pizzapizza.vze.com, 11:30 A.M.–9 P.M. daily except Wednesday), on Calle Centenario at 5 Avenida NE, serves up a tasty pizza pie, as well as grinders, spaghetti, and garlic bread, all at reasonable prices. There is a book exchange and a kids' play area in the courtyard. The restaurant does not serve beer.

Weekend's Pizza (4 Av. and 2 Calle SO, tel. 504/2662-4121, 9 A.M.–9 P.M. Tues.–Sun.) is owned by a former Peace Corps volunteer and her Honduran husband. They drive to San Pedro Sula weekly to bring back ingredients you can't find anywhere in Santa Rosa, such as Gouda cheese and sun-dried tomatoes. Many locals claim they serve the best pizza in Honduras here.

Although it is due to move locations at any time and so we couldn't put it on the map, we had to be sure to include **La Gondola** (noon–2 P.M. and 6–10 P.M. Mon.–Sat.), owned by an Italian-loving Honduran woman. Serving a combination of pastas and protein-based main courses, she has traditional dishes like chicken Milanese and pasta *amatriciana*, as well as some dishes with a local twist, such as pasta copán with *loroco*, pasta in a sauce with small flowers (US$8–12). Ask around for the current location, or call 504/9848-5227 to double-check.

At the time of writing, **Las Brasas Steak House** (11:30 A.M.–10 P.M. daily) had just opened a branch of its popular meat-focused restaurant in Santa Rosa. The most elegant restaurant in town, it offers a combination of national and imported beef, mixed grills, and a small selection of ceviches and other seafood dishes. Prices range from US$8 for an 8-ounce Honduran tenderloin, to US$27 for a 16-ounce skirt steak. If you're there midday, ask about their lunch discount.

INFORMATION AND SERVICES
Banks

Banco de Occidente is the best for exchanging dollars and travelers checks, while **Banco Atlántida** has a cash machine at its branch by the bus terminal, in the new shopping center with the 20 Menos supermarket. Cash advances on a Visa card are available at Banco Atlántida and BGA.

Communications

Hondutel (7 A.M.–9 P.M. daily) and **Honducor** are next to each other on the west side of the park.

For Internet access, several places downtown have computers, including **Bonsay Cyber Café** (9 A.M.–9 P.M. Mon.–Sat., noon–7 P.M. Sun.), where you can get a *granita* with your Internet. There is also Internet access available at the tourism kiosk in the main square.

Laundry

At **Lavandería Wash and Dry**, on 1 Calle NE, half a block from Plaza Saavedra, laundry is a steep US$5 a load.

Spanish Schools

Should the climes and friendly feel of Santa Rosa tempt you to stay awhile, you could fill your time taking Spanish classes at the **Santa Rosa de Copán Language School** (tel. 504/2662-1378, www.spanish-ili-copan.com). Santa Rosa would certainly be a relaxing place to spend a few weeks or months studying, and unlike in Antigua, Guatemala, you wouldn't speak a whole lot of English in your free time. Classes are US$250 for 20 hours of instruction in a week (minimum two weeks), which can be solo, or you can share the cost and classes with up to four more people. Homestays are sometimes available.

Emergencies

If you have an emergency, you may find the following numbers helpful: **policía**, tel. 504/2662-0091 or 504/2662-0308, or dial 199; **fire department**, tel. 504/2662-1719, or dial 198; **Red Cross** (for an ambulance), tel. 504/2662-0045, or dial 195; and the **hospital**, tel. 504/2662-0128 or 504/662-0093.

GETTING THERE AND AROUND
Bus

Unless otherwise noted, all buses depart from the main bus terminal on the San Pedro Sula highway about one kilometer north of town. Taxis between the terminal and downtown cost US$0.80, although sometimes you take a scenic tour dropping off other passengers on the way into town.

To **Gracias, Lempira Express** (tel. 504/9888-7919) has frequent buses, the first departing at 5:30 A.M. (US$2.60, about 70 minutes). Several of these buses continue on to **La Esperanza** (US$6.30, about 3.5 hours).

To **Ocotepeque, Sultana** (tel. 504/2662-0940) runs hourly buses starting at 2 P.M., with the last departing at 8 P.M., charging US$4.20. **Toritos y Coanpecos** and **Congolón** run buses on the same route, but starting at 8:30 A.M., with service to Agua Caliente at the border (US$8.20).

To **San Pedro Sula, Toritos y Copanecos** runs direct buses hourly between 6 A.M. and 5 P.M., US$5.25) and are worth planning on. Regular buses start at 4 A.M. and cost US$4.20, but take an extra hour. **Congolón** has similar service, but charges US$5.80.

To **Copán Ruinas,** take a bus to La Entrada and catch another bus or a *rapidito* on to Copán Ruinas.

To **Corquín,** eight buses depart daily between 8 A.M. and midafternoon (US$2.25, one hour).

To **Belén Gualcho,** there are two buses a day at 10:30 A.M. and 11:30 A.M. (US$2.50, about three hours).

Car

The highways to La Entrada (44 kilometers), San Pedro Sula (170 kilometers), Gracias (47 kilometers), and Nueva Ocotepeque (92 kilometers) are all paved and well maintained, although a good rainy season can make a liar out of anyone.

NEAR SANTA ROSA DE COPÁN

A portion of the old *camino real,* now a dirt road, passes near Santa Rosa, beginning in the village of San Agustín, beyond Dulce Nombre de Copán. From here you can walk over the crest of the mountains down to Santa Rita, near Copán Ruinas, in a day. It's also fairly easy to catch a *jalón* on a passing pickup truck along the scenic road, which comes out by Hacienda El Jaral, just north of Santa Rita.

Near the *camino real,* on the south side, close to the highest point in the road, is the privately owned **Monte Quetzal,** a 1,900-meter mountain with dense cedar forest and plenty of its avian namesakes flitting among the trees. On the top of the mountain is a lush fern forest. An old mine, abandoned in 1965, can be explored up to 200 meters into the hillside. Max Elvir of Lenca Travel knows the owner and can arrange trips there for US$25 a day per person for a small group. Although the mountain is rich with its namesake birds, quetzals are notoriously difficult to spot, but with a bit of luck and patience, you just might see the long-tailed bird. Easier to spot are the countless centennial trees, including cedar, liquidambar (American sweet gum), oak, and calabash.

Sixteen kilometers from Santa Rosa on the San Pedro highway is a dirt road turnoff to the east leading to **Quezailica,** a small town centered around the beautiful **Santuario del Milagroso Cristo Negro, El Señor del Buen Fin,** built in 1660 and declared a national monument in 1987. In the church is a carved wooden Cristo Negro (Black Christ), made by an unknown artist who was apparently a student of famed sculptor Quirio Cataño, who made the Cristo Negro of Esquipulas. A major Chortí Mayan community in pre-Columbian times, this area contains many relics of the Chortí Maya, including an odd rock monolith carved in the shape of a face, which was found hidden in the church's atrium and is now sitting outside the church. One bus drives to Quezailica from Santa Rosa at 1 P.M., every day but Sunday. You can also take any bus to La Entrada and get off at the turnoff to San José. From there you can either catch a *rapidito* or walk the seven kilometers to Quezailica.

The town festival, on January 15, is a major event for the entire region. Pilgrims follow an old *camino real* to the church and the Cristo Negro, with some 50,000 people visiting in a period of five days. Max Elvir of Lenca Travel has arranged a tour that costs US$10, providing transportation to the village of Las Sandías, from where visitors walk on an old *camino real* the 1.5–2 hours to Quezailica. Max will drop avid hikers in Belén for a longer walk that meets up with the other visitors in Las Sandías.

Belén Gualcho

Accessible by dirt road from Santa Rosa de Copán via Cucuyagua and Corquín, high on the side of the Sierra de Celaque, is the mountain town of Belén Gualcho. The town is dominated by a well-maintained, triple-domed colonial-era church, among the most beautiful in the country. Great views of the church are had from the local grade school—the guard will usually let you in if you ask nicely.

The town hosts a large **Sunday market,** which attracts campesinos from the mountain villages and is quite a colorful and lively event, well worth scheduling your trip to see. It's pretty much done by 11 A.M., so if you want to see it, you have to get there the night before, and best to be early on Saturday before the hotels fill up.

Belén's annual festival is held on January 17 in honor of San Antonio de Abad. The story goes that in years past, a spirit was so impressed by Belén's festival that every year he arrived on a black mule and took part in the revelry himself, afterward disappearing into the hills. But one year, a group of young men thought it would be amusing to attach a bunch of firecrackers to the mule's tail. Offended by this evident lack of respect for his otherworldliness, the spirit—known as El Hombre de Belén Gualcho—rode off in a huff and has never returned.

A comfortable hotel in Belén is **Hotelito El Carmen** (no phone, US$3–7), with 20 clean rooms. Bathrooms are communal, and no hot water is available. Some private rooms are available for a bit more. Don't come out here expecting luxury. Similar although less clean is **Hotel Olvin** (US$4–7, the pricier rooms with private bath). Both hotels are often full on Saturday nights, as people arrive for the Sunday market, but other rooms can often be found by asking around, particularly in the stores.

Of the local eateries in town, **Comedor Raquel** serves good, inexpensive *típico* food in a friendly little dining room.

There's a small Internet shop open daily next to Hotel Olvin.

It's easy to combine a visit to **Corquín** with a trip to Belén Gualcho. Corquín is an attractive colonial village, and there are waterfalls nearby. Both *comida típica* and tourist information are available at **La Casa Grande Restaurante**, located in a colonial house in town.

One bus travels daily between Belén and Santa Rosa de Copán, via Cucayagua and Corquín, leaving Santa Rosa at 1 P.M. There are also buses that go between San Pedro Sula and Belén Gualcho, passing Santa Rosa at 10 A.M. and 2 P.M., reaching Corquín in another 1.5–2 hours and Belén Gualcho another 45 minutes after that. Alternatively, you can catch the more frequent buses to Corquín and try to hitch from there, though pickups are often full already. The schedule for buses back to Santa Rosa from Belén (US$2) varies, but they all leave early in the morning, the exception being Sunday, when the last buses leave at midday. If coming by car, the turn to Corquín and Belén Gualcho is off the Santa Rosa–Nueva Ocotepeque highway, 16 miles from Santa Rosa. Be forewarned that the 24-kilometer stretch between Corquín and Belén Gualcho can be pretty challenging, best for a four-wheel drive.

Lepaera

Heading south toward Gracias, about 45 minutes from Santa Rosa, is the town of Lepaera. Settled in 1538, Lepaera is one of the oldest settlements in the area, although it wasn't granted the title of city until 1956. Be sure to take note of the town church, which, according the inscription over its entrance, dates from July 28, 1640.

Lepaera is in the foothills of the Puca mountain, and guides in town can take travelers on a visit to the cloud forests of the **Refugio de Vida Silvestre Puca**. The high elevation is perfect for coffee, and plantations in the area are booming.

The **Hotel Murillo** (tel. 504/2655-5383, US$12 s, US$18 d) offers rooms with private bath.

There are several spots in town where tourists can buy homemade ground coffee, known as *café de palo*. Coffee from Gregorio Martinez's farm took first prize at a national "Cup of Excellence" competition in 2004.

The town's holidays are January 25, in honor of the Señor de Esquipulas, and July 25, in honor of Santiago (Saint James).

To get to Lepaera by car from Santa Rosa, take the turnoff a couple of kilometers after Las Flores (in between two tight curves), about 15 kilometers before Gracias.

Gracias and the Lenca Highlands

One of the natural and cultural treasures of Honduras, the mountain country between Gracias, La Esperanza, and the Salvadoran border is a beautiful region of pine forest and infrequently visited colonial villages. Foreign tourists who make it to the town of Gracias and to the nearby Sierra de Celaque, a national park boasting the country's highest peak, are rewarded with thoughtful opportunities for community tourism, constantly improving amenities for accommodations and food, and spectacular scenery.

The dirt roads and trails connecting the highland villages of Belén Gualcho, La Campa, San Manuel Colohete, Erandique, and beyond are lovely places to lose yourself for days at a time, admiring the colonial villages seemingly long-forgotten in their secluded corners of the rugged countryside. The Lenca campesinos populating the region are extremely friendly, and although some might wonder what you're doing out there, the worst that will happen is you'll be invited in for so many cups of coffee you'll never get anywhere and end up all jittery on caffeine.

Those who spend time in this region should try to keep a certain sensitivity to the realities and customs of the campesinos who inhabit the countryside. One is expected to stop and greet others met on the trail, at least with a gentle handshake (none of those U.S. finger-breaking grips, please) and a friendly hello. You are not, of course, required to stop, have coffee, and talk at every home you pass, but always offer a polite decline. It's worth accepting the invitation once in a while. You never know—a conversation with a campesino family out in the mountains of Honduras, asking about their lives and telling them about yours, may end up being one of your most memorable travel experiences. Try to take it with aplomb when you are surrounded and pursued relentlessly by a dozen local kids.

Tours

In Gracias, the **tourist office** (www.colosuca.com) has developed excellent tourist information for the **Colosuca Tourist Circuit**—the region encompassing Parque Nacional Celaque, the town of Gracias, and the villages of La Campa, San Manuel Colohete, San Marcos de Caiquín, San Sebastián, and Belén (that's Belén, Lempira, not Belén Gualcho, Ocotepeque).

The **Asociación de Guías Turísticos Colosuca-Celaque** has 15 community guides (with limited English) available for tours in Gracias, Celaque, and the surrounding villages. They can also arrange trips on horses (US$12 per hour per person, plus US$12 for the guide). Other tours (city tour, Lencan villages, hiking, coffee) cost US$45 for three hours; for tours of 3–6 hours, the charge is US$75 and includes lunch. The coordinator of the association is Marco Aurelio Rodríguez (tel. 504/2656-0627 or 9870-8821, guiamarcolencas@yahoo.com). Marco is the owner of El Jarrón restaurant at the corner of the central square, so you can try stopping by for information. Both guide outfits can help arrange camping gear if you don't have any.

The Hotel Guancascos can also put you in touch with other city guides, such as Paulino Portillo, while the more adventurous can contact Antonio Melgar (tel. 504/9998-5251) and his brother Candido (tel. 504/9971-5114) for long hikes in Celaque. Two-day trips to Cerro de las Minas cost US$53, while four day trips across the mountain to the exit leading to Belén Gualcho run US$160.

◖ GRACIAS

A sleepy colonial town, its days of glory as the capital of Central America more than four centuries in the past, Gracias makes a great base to explore this beautiful region of western Honduras. Formerly just a destination for

mototaxis at Gracias's parque central

backpackers, Gracias is these days attracting more tourists of all varieties, drawn by the town's colonial architecture; the cloud forest atop the Celaque mountain range, southwest of town; and nearby Lenca villages, including La Campa and San Manuel Colohete.

Summer in the area is March and April, when it can get quite hot and air-conditioning becomes a good investment. Not even a fan is necessary for a visit October through January.

History

Founded in the earliest phase of the conquest of Honduras, Gracias a Dios was relocated twice before being established at its current location on January 14, 1539, by Bishop Cristóbal de Pedraza and Juan de Montejo under orders of Francisco de Montejo, then ruler of Honduras. In those early years, the would-be colonists were engaged in a fierce struggle against the Lenca leader Lempira, and the settlement was apparently moved for strategic reasons. The second location reportedly served as the main Spanish base for quelling the revolt, after which the town was moved farther south to its present location.

According to legend, the town received its name because one of the conquistadors had a heck of a time finding any land flat enough for a town in the mountainous region. When a suitable spot was located, the Spaniards reportedly gave the heartfelt cry, "Thank God we've finally found flat land!" Hence, Gracias a Dios (later shortened to "Gracias").

With the establishment of the Audiencia de los Confines in Gracias on May 16, 1544, the town became the administrative center of Central America. The *audiencia* was a royal court of sorts with power to impart civil and criminal justice and a jurisdiction ranging from the Yucatán to Panama. Some of the larger towns in Guatemala and El Salvador quickly became jealous of the prestige accorded Gracias and forced the *audiencia* to move to Antigua, Guatemala, in late 1548.

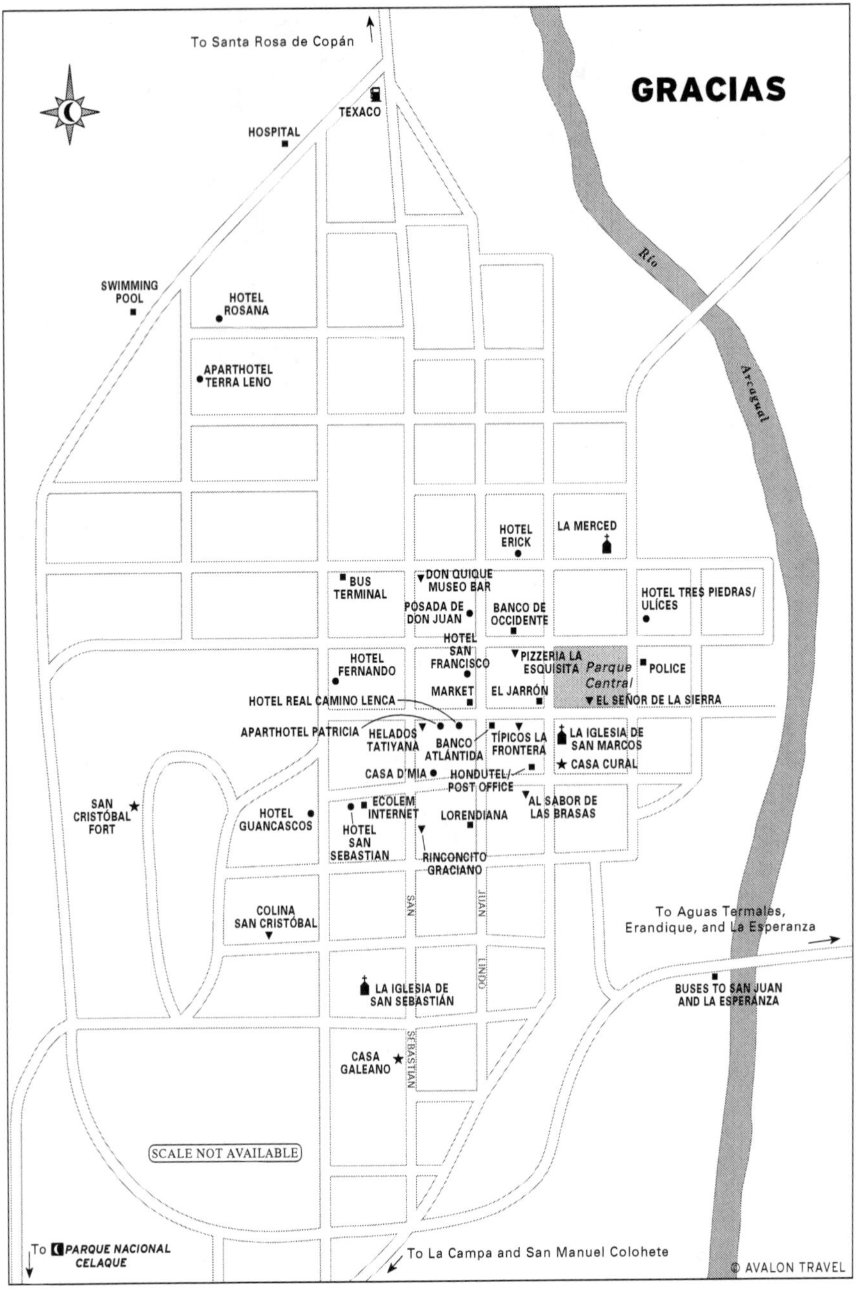
GRACIAS
To Santa Rosa de Copán
TEXACO
HOSPITAL
SWIMMING POOL
HOTEL ROSANA
APARTHOTEL TERRA LENO
Río Arcagual
HOTEL ERICK
LA MERCED
BUS TERMINAL
DON QUIQUE MUSEO BAR
POSADA DE DON JUAN
BANCO DE OCCIDENTE
HOTEL TRES PIEDRAS/ULÍCES
HOTEL SAN FRANCISCO
HOTEL FERNANDO
PIZZERIA LA ESQUISITA
Parque Central
POLICE
MARKET
EL JARRÓN
EL SEÑOR DE LA SIERRA
HOTEL REAL CAMINO LENCA
APARTHOTEL PATRICIA
HELADOS TATIYANA
BANCO ATLÁNTIDA
TÍPICOS LA FRONTERA
LA IGLESIA DE SAN MARCOS
CASA CURAL
CASA D'MIA
HONDUTEL/POST OFFICE
SAN CRISTÓBAL FORT
HOTEL GUANCASCOS
ECOLEM INTERNET
HOTEL SAN SEBASTIAN
LORENDIANA
AL SABOR DE LAS BRASAS
RINCONCITO GRACIANO
COLINA SAN CRISTÓBAL
SAN JUAN LINDO
To Aguas Termales, Erandique, and La Esperanza
LA IGLESIA DE SAN SEBASTIÁN
BUSES TO SAN JUAN AND LA ESPERANZA
SAN SEBASTIAN
CASA GALEANO
SCALE NOT AVAILABLE
To PARQUE NACIONAL CELAQUE
To La Campa and San Manuel Colohete
© AVALON TRAVEL

La Merced, a 400-year-old church in Gracias

Following the removal of the *audiencia,* Gracias fell into a long, slow slide. When the little gold and silver in the area were quickly worked within a couple of decades after the conquest, local colonists had little to fall back on beyond cattle ranching and tobacco production. Gracias remained an important administrative center for Honduras throughout the colonial period, but by the early 19th century, nearby Santa Rosa de Copán had taken over the tobacco industry and, not long after, also became the de facto regional capital.

Over the past decade, Gracias has worked hard (and successfully) to put itself back on the map through the development of a tourist industry. Capitalizing on the rich human and natural resources in the region, the town has established itself as a premier base for travelers looking for that elusive travel experience—approachable authenticity.

Sights

Of the four churches in Gracias, **La Merced,** a block north of the *parque* (square) is the most historic. Construction on its ornate sculpted facade began in 1611 and lasted 30 years. It is open on Saturday, when mass is held. The main church on the *parque,* **La Iglesia de San Marcos,** was built in 1715, and was recently renovated (along with the whole square). The interior is simple, but the carved wooden icons in the alcoves along the walls are worth a look. Next door, formerly used as the *casa cural* (priests' house) and now housing a radio station, is the building that once housed the Audiencia de los Confines.

In the center of a shady square a few blocks southwest of the main square is **La Iglesia de San Sebastián,** also known as La Ermita. Built in 1930, the exterior at least is in good condition—it's hard to know anything about the interior, since the church only opens for a mass once a year, on its namesake day (January 20, commemorating the death of Saint Sebastian). Gracias has four churches but currently only one priest. The surrounding park is basically a dirt lot, but it has some decent play equipment if you are toting kids.

On the east side of La Ermita is the **Casa Galeano** (9 A.M.–6 P.M. daily, US$1.60), the former colonial residence of a prominent longtime Gracias family. Nicely restored with the help of the Spanish government, the Casa Galeano now houses a simple museum on the region, worth the small admission fee for a quick look. Admission also includes entry to the unimpressive botanical garden behind the house.

The Galeano family now resides in another building, and Eduardo "Mito" Galeano is a respected Honduran painter who will sometimes show visitors samples of his work—ask around to find his nearby workshop. Many of Galeano's paintings take as their subject matter village life in western Honduras.

Perched on a hill just west of downtown, the **San Cristóbal fort** was built in the mid-19th century as an afterthought to the turbulence raging across Central America in earlier decades. In spite of its impressive construction, the fort never saw any action and now fills with families on outings and lounging teens on a Sunday afternoon. The fort was the idea of Honduran and Salvadoran president Juan Lindo (he served 1847–1852), and it was built around his tomb six years after his death. In addition to admiring the two cannons (brought from the fort at Omoa), a good reason to visit is to check out the views across Gracias, the surrounding countryside, and Sierra de Celaque looming up to the southwest. The fort's gates are open 7 A.M.–5 P.M. daily. Reach it by climbing the stairs next to Hotel Guancasco, or hiring a *mototaxi* for US$0.60 per person.

Gracias's fourth church is **La Iglesia de Santa Lucía,** two kilometers down the road toward the Celaque visitors center.

Entertainment and Events

Thanks to its four churches, Gracias celebrates four *ferias patronales* a year: January 20 (San Sebastián), April 25 (San Marcos), September 28 (La Merced), and December 13 (Santa Lucía). Of special note are the unique **guancascos** that take place during the January and December festivities. A *guancasco* is a traditional masked dance representing peace and communication between two communities. In Gracias, the neighborhoods of San Sebastián and Mexicapa (by the church of Santa Lucía) reenact this encounter.

On July 20 the town commemorates the death of the Lencan hero Lempira, with hundreds of schoolchildren parading in Indian-style costumes and a reenactment of Lenca's betrayal and death, an event well worth observing if you're anywhere nearby on that day.

It bears noting that Gracias has virtually no nightlife and is proud of its quiet, small-town nature. Your best bet after dinner is a beer at the terrace of **Hotel Guancascos** for some conversation and a view, or a drink at **Kandil,** half a block east from Guancascos. Braver souls can check out **Don Quique Museo Bar**, which has an interesting array of antique arms and pictures for decor, and friendly owners, but the place opens at 9 A.M. and serves only drinks, no food, so the crowd can be pretty rowdy by evening. If you're female and traveling solo, you might be able to have a drink midday without trouble if you want, but we don't suggest that females alone or female-only groups come by in the evening.

Shopping

Although small, the gift shop at **El Jarrón** (at the corner of the *parque central*) probably offers the best selection of souvenirs in town, ranging from tourist kitsch to well-made Lencan pottery made by women in La Campa.

A visit to ◖ **Lorendiana** (7 A.M.–7 P.M. daily) is a must, if only to admire the eye-catching displays of pickled onions, chilies, and other vegetables, jars of blackberry, mango, strawberry, and even pineapple with jalapeño jams, and bottles of fruit wine. Candies made with *dulce de leche* mixed with vanilla (yum!) or with nance fruit (gag!) are available, or satisfy your sweet tooth with a homemade popsicle from one of the giant freezers. Flavors include mango, milk with cinnamon, and blackberry, to name just a few of the dozen or so varieties. Lorendiana also sells some small handicrafts such as corn husk dolls and tiny Lencan pots. Stock up on the gift bags of handmade paper and some candies or jam to bring home.

Recreation

The perfect remedy for limbs aching from all that traveling, especially if you've just slogged up to the top of Sierra de Celaque, is a visit to the *aguas termales*.

The cheapies are about five kilometers east of Gracias, a couple of bumpy kilometers off the road to La Esperanza. The first set, Las Marias, has three stone pools—one at 40°C (104°F), the other two at 37°C (99°F)—built around the springs, surrounded by large trees and thick vegetation. One of the pools is long enough to take a few swimming strokes across, a very pleasurable experience in the warm water. A small restaurant at the pools serves up soft drinks, beers, and snacks and meals, and a barbecue pit is available for rent.

The second set of four pools, Presidente, is a bit lower down, and pleasant but not quite as warm. There is one shallow pool perfect for kids, and at the pool off to the right ask the locals to show you the sulfur stone that can be crushed on the spot into a facial mask. The lower pools have a snack bar selling chips, sodas, and beer, as well as changing rooms and restrooms. Bring your own towels. Both sets of pools are open 5 A.M.–11 P.M. or later daily and cost US$1.50. Reputedly there will soon be massages available here.

To get there without a car, hire a *mototaxi* for US$3 (one way), hitch a ride up the La Esperanza road to the turnoff, or start walking up the road and keep an eye out for a path heading off to the right—a shortcut to the pools, just past the second bridge outside of town. It takes about 90 minutes walking by the road and about an hour by the trail—or just 10 minutes if you have your own wheels.

Alternatively, head seven kilometers toward Santa Rosa de Copán to reach **Termas del Río** (5 A.M.–11 P.M. daily, US$5.25), a complex that offers nature trails, horseback rides, children's play equipment, massages, barbecue pits, and handicapped access, in addition to the pools.

In addition to the fantastic hiking on Sierra de Celaque, there are a number of **trails** in the foothills near Gracias. A trail map is available at the Hotel Guancascos, indicating paths that lead to the thermal baths or through the *aldeas* (villages) around Gracias.

Horseback riding can be arranged through Hotel Guancascos, US$42 for one person, US$53 for two, and US$21 per person for three or more, including transportation and a guide.

Accommodations
UNDER US$25

Travelers looking to save their lempiras should head directly to **Hotel Erick** (tel. 504/2656-1066, angelcar@yahoo.com, US$16 s/d with hot water, US$10.50 s/d without), one block north of the square, which has spotless if bare-bones rooms.

The modern **Hotel San Francisco** (tel. 504/2656-0078, US$21 s and US$26 d with fan, US$31.50 s/d with a/c), above a shop a block west of the *parque central,* has spacious, travel lodge–style rooms with cable TV and nice bathrooms, but old sheets and no wireless Internet. The windows in rooms 1 and 2 face out toward the parking lot, street, and hills, while the windows of all the other rooms face the interior hall.

Joining the ranks of budget-friendly hotels in Gracias is **Casa D'Mia Hotel** (US$21 s, US$24 d). Rooms are fairly spacious, which perhaps

one of Gracias's small colonial hotels

adds to their slightly barren feel, but they are cheered up by colorful walls (pink, yellow, green). All the rooms have wireless Internet access and TVs. What they don't have is air-conditioning, and these rooms are on the hot side, so keep that in mind for travel in March or April, Honduras's summer months.

Around the corner from Hotel Guancascos, conveniently located next door to an Internet café, is **Hotel San Sebastián** (tel. 504/2656-0398, hotel-sansebastian@yahoo.com, US$16 s, US$24 d). The eight simple rooms have wireless Internet, air-conditioning, TVs, and acceptable bathrooms with hot water.

A few blocks out from the center of town is **Hotel Rosario** (tel. 504/2656-0694, US$21 s/d with fan, US$37 s/d with a/c), with 29 rooms encircling a parking lot. The rooms are clean, although the cheaper ones have old linens and some lack a shower head. The pricier rooms are on the second floor, newly painted, and some have king beds.

US$25-50

The most popular digs in town are at **Hotel Guancascos** (tel. 504/2656-1219, www.guancascos.com, US$21 s, US$29 d), three blocks west and one block south of the *parque central,* offering 17 rooms tastefully built in a rustic style, each with hot water, cable TV, fan, and a large window. Banana trees and other plants grow around the grounds. Rooms 7, 8, and 9, under the restaurant, have beautiful views, but noise from the restaurant wafts down, so they aren't the best choice for those who like to hit the sack early. The hotel is noteworthy for being one of just two hotels in the country certified for sustainable tourism (the other being Casa del Arbol in San Pedro Sula). The restaurant is a good place to meet other travelers in Gracias and to gather tourist information, and it has a computer with free Internet access for hotel guests to use. Guancascos also rents sleeping bags (US$2) and tents (US$5–10), and can arrange outings on horseback.

A very good value on the outskirts of town is **Finca El Capitán** (tel. 504/2656-1659, US$21 s, US$37 d), facing the Santa Lucía church on the road that leads to Celaque. The 20 rooms are spaced through 12 cabins painted in rose, peach, and teal, encircling a large common area with grass and banana trees, a swimming pool, and children's play area. Beds have colonial-style dark-wood headboards, and the cabin porches have hammocks and rocking chairs in which to while away an afternoon. There is a full-service restaurant (breakfast US$2.50–3.50, dinner US$4–6), decorated with hollow gourds and animal hides.

A recent addition to Gracias is **Hotel Tres Piedras** (tel. 504/2656-0870, www.trespiedrashotel.com, US$23 s, US$33 d), a two-story building tucked behind shops and restaurants just half a block from the park. Rooms face a courtyard of stone and plants, and have wireless Internet, TVs, fans, and nice linens. It's not fancy, but a very good value for the price. The one drawback: Since the reception area is right in the courtyard, which the rooms surround, anyone talking there, or a TV that is switched on early in the morning, is audible in every room of the hotel.

The much simpler **Aparthotel Patricia** (tel. 504/2656-1281, US$32 s/d) is another acceptable option, with five spacious rooms with tiled bathrooms, air-conditioning, and cable TV. The hotel has one very large apartment for US$42, with two bedrooms and a full kitchen. The furnishings are nothing special, but if space is what you need, Patricia's got it.

Apart Hotel Tierra Lenca (tel. 504/2656-1540, US$42 s/d) trades space for style. The units are smaller, but new and well-equipped with a microwave, fridge, sink, air-conditioning, and TV. The hotel is a few blocks away from the center of town, and the sign can be a little hard to spot, especially at night. If there is no one in reception, try 504/9802-0165.

By the Presidente thermal baths is **Villas del Agua Caliente** (tel. 504/9976-1654 or 9715-8523, hotel.villasdelaguacaliente@hotmail.com, US$24 s, US$37 d), with 16 rooms in three cabins, plus a restaurant. The cabins have ochre stucco walls and exposed beams, as well as a fan and TV; some rooms can accommodate up to six. The pools are fun to visit at night, and after a few hours in the pools, with a couple of beers, having a bed nearby is not such a bad idea.

Outside of town is the group-friendly **Villa de Ada** (tel. 504/2656-1310, US$34 s, US$45 d), with twelve square cabins set near lagoons. There are swimming pools for adults and children, and it's possible to take a boat ride or fish in the lagoon (the restaurant is renowned for its fried tilapia).

The ◖ **Hotel Real Camino Lenca** (tel. 504/2656-1712, www.hotelrealcaminolenca.com) is a nice high-end addition to the range of accommodations in Gracias, with luxury touches: flat-screen TVs and wireless Internet, quality linens, good bathroom fixtures, towels rolled into the form of swans at the end of each bed. The 14 rooms are set around a small atrium, and the hotel has a restaurant and a sleek rooftop bar, offers laundry service, and can arrange a guide for visitors who want to explore the city and surrounding area. The fancy cloth shower curtains are already showing signs of age, but overall it's a nice hotel and a good value. Prices range from US$40–50, according to the number of beds and the amenities (a/c and hydro-massage showers being the perks). Breakfast is included in the price.

US$50-100

The swankiest place in town is **Posada de Don Juan** (tel. 504/2656-1020, www.posadadedonjuanhotel.com), with luxury linens and flat-screen TVs, as well as a good restaurant, swimming pool, parking, and wireless Internet. The best (and priciest) rooms are the deluxe rooms around the pool (US$78 s, US$91 d, US$110 t); the others encircle the parking lot motel-style, have fans instead of air-conditioning, full-size beds instead of queen, and are fine, but not quite as well maintained (US$48 s, US$60 d, US$91 t).

Food

Restaurante Guancascos (tel. 504/2656-1219, 7 A.M.–10 P.M. daily) has cornered the market on travelers, and it's easy to see why. The restaurant, with a fine view over Gracias and the surrounding countryside, is run by a knowledgeable Dutch woman, Fronica, who offers Honduran standards at reasonable prices. Something vegetarian is always available. Breakfasts run US$2.50–5.25, dishes like *baleadas,* tacos, nachos, sandwiches, and the "vegetarian plate" run US$2.25–4.50, and main dishes such as pasta are US$5.25–10. The food might take a while to arrive, so relax with a couple of beers and talk with other travelers about the many places to see around Gracias. Books and handicrafts are for sale, camping gear for Celaque hikes can be rented here, and Fronica can help you arrange a ride to the park, a guide, horseback riding, and the like. You can also look at topographical maps for the area, although they aren't for sale.

Rinconcito Graciano (tel. 504/2656-1171) serves both creative and traditional Lenca dishes with all-natural ingredients in an atmospheric environment with wood tables and Lencan decor. The chicken in a *loroco*-spinach-mushroom sauce is delicious, as are the fruit juices and *atoles* that come served in cups made of gourds. Unfortunately, the service doesn't match the concept, portions can be small, and the restaurant doesn't seem to hold regular hours. The *artesanías* adorning the walls are all locally made.

El Jarrón (tel. 504/2656-0668), in new digs on the corner of the park, has low-priced *desayunos* and *cenas* (US$2.50–4) as well as a special "Jarrón-style soup"—cream of corn with chunks of beef, chicken, or pork, served with rice and tortillas (US$2)—snacks like *baleadas,* and tacos. There is a small shop with *artesanías* and coffee as well. Owner Marco Aurelio Rodriguez (tel. 504/2656-0627 or 9870-8821, guiamarcolencas@yahoo.com) is a local guide, and he has a van available if you need transportation.

Just across the street is **Típicos La Frontera** (7 A.M.–10 P.M. Mon.–Sat., 8 A.M.–2 P.M. Sun.), with a similar selection of *baleadas,* tacos, nachos, and *almuerzos* (US$0.60–3.50). The menu here has English too, for those who have been struggling to decipher Spanish menus.

Specializing in soups and grilled meats is **Al Sabor de Las Brasas** ("with the taste of coals") (tel. 504/2655-9791, 7 A.M.–9 P.M. Mon.–Sat., 7 A.M.–1 P.M. Sun.). Soups (US$4–5) vary but might include beef, seafood, bean, or *mondogo,* and there is *gallina india* (Indian hen) daily. Meats on offer (US$5.25 each) include beef loin, pork loin, skirt steak, Argentinian sausage, liver, pork ribs and chops, as well as a mixed grill (US$21, serves 3–4 people). Breakfasts are hearty as well, *típico,* or *huevos a la ranchera* (US$3–4).

Pizza with a thick, crispy crust and smothered in cheese is the specialty at **Colina San Cristóbal** (7 A.M.–10 P.M. daily), a tableclothed restaurant near San Sebastián church. The small (US$7–9.50) makes for two generous portions. Burgers, fish, and the standard *comida típica* are available as well (US$3.50–7). The cheaper and much more basic **Pizzeria y Repostería La Esquisita** is always hopping with locals, and offers cake to go with your pizza.

Mesón de Don Juan at the Posada de Don Juan hotel has all the usual suspects, plus items like French toast and omelets for breakfast (US$3–4), as well as *churrasco* (Argentine-style grilled beef, US$8) and pasta (US$7–11) for dinner.

For bargain eats, head to the street corner by the Posada de Don Juan, where women set up charcoal barbecues in the evenings. You can stock up on supplies at the mini grocery store **Super El Milagro.**

Coffee and Snacks

The kiosk in the park is home to **El Señor de la Sierra,** where you can pick up a cappuccino or a *granita de café* to sit and enjoy on a park bench. Facing the park is **KOBS/La Casita del Pastel,** the place to go if your craving is not for coffee, but for sweets like ice cream or cake.

Fresh fruits and vegetables are for sale in front of the bus terminal for Lempira Express.

Information and Services

Excellent tourist information is available through the regional website www.colosuca.com. Tourist information and a sketch map of the Celaque trails can also be found at Restaurante Guancascos.

Banco de Occidente, a block west of the square, changes dollars and travelers checks, and has an ATM. Western Union funds can be received here, and there is also a branch of Banco Atlántida if you need to receive a MoneyGram.

Hondutel (7 A.M.–9 P.M. daily) and **Honducor** are a block south of the square. Lower-priced international calls can be made at **Ecolem Internet** (8 A.M.–8 P.M. Mon.–Sat.), along with Internet access for US$1 per hour. There are several other Internet places in town; **Ulices**, near the park, has similar prices and hours.

The local police station is at the edge of the square (tel. 504/2656-1036). If, heaven forbid, you have a health emergency, head to the Hospital Juan M. Gálvez (tel. 504/2656-1100).

Getting There and Away

Copanecos (tel. 504/2662-2572) and **Coop. Trans. Ltd.** (tel. 504/2656-1214) have buses to Santa Rosa de Copán between 6 A.M. and 6 P.M., with a departure every half hour or so between the two companies (60 minutes, US$2.15).

The 77-kilometer road from Gracias via San Juan to La Esperanza is slowly, very slowly, being paved. Work has gone on for years, and it is now paved for all but the 13 kilometers closest to La Esperanza. Of course, the first portion of the road to have been paved, between Gracias and San Juan, is now full of potholes. But it is a very beautiful drive through pine-forested country, and the quickest way to Siguatepeque, Comayagua, Tegucigalpa, and all points south, instead of returning toward Santa Rosa and San Pedro Sula.

One bus leaves Gracias daily from the bridge southeast of town at 5 A.M. for the 2.5-hour ride to La Esperanza (US$4), connecting to the direct bus to Tegucigalpa. (This bus heads back to Gracias at 11 A.M.) The *busitos* (minibuses) to San Juan are hourly, and from there you can get another bus onward to La Esperanza (also hourly).

Lempira Express (tel. 504/9888-7919) runs between Gracias and Santa Rosa de Copán every 40 minutes, charging US$2.65 for direct service and US$2.35 for regular service. The first buses depart at 5:30 A.M., and the last around 5:30 P.M. Some of the buses from Santa Rosa to Gracias also continue on to La Esperanza.

One bus a day goes to Erandique at noon (four hours, US$2). Hitchhiking is also usually possible; look for the flatbed trucks carrying other passengers as well, but don't get into a private car. A couple of buses also go this way to the Salvadoran border.

There are four buses daily to San Pedro Sula, all leaving in the morning (between 5 A.M. and 9 A.M.). **Gracianos** (tel. 504/2656-1403) has buses to San Pedro Sula at 6 A.M. and 8:50 A.M.

From San Pedro, there are three buses: Cooperativa Transportes Lempira (tel. 504/2656-1214) at 1 P.M.; Gracianos (tel. 504/2656-1403) at 11 A.M. and 2 P.M.; and Toritos (tel. 504/2662-0156 or 504/2516-2086 in San Pedro) at 3 P.M., charging US$5.25–5.75. If these schedules don't work for you, your other option is to connect via Santa Rosa de Copán.

There is limited bus service between Gracias and the surrounding Lenca villages. Each has one bus per day each direction; check the tourist office website at www.colosuca.com (click on "How to Get There") for details. It is probably easier to get a *jalón,* a ride in the bed of a pickup. Many travelers prefer to use Gracias as a base, to take advantage of the city's hotels and restaurants, but each of the villages has at least a *comedor,* and a few simple, small hotels as well. If you don't mind the limited creature comforts, the villages offer unique opportunities to experience Honduran mountain life.

◖ PARQUE NACIONAL CELAQUE

One of the premier natural protected areas in Honduras, Celaque boasts the country's highest mountain, Cerro de las Minas, at 2,849 meters, as well as an impressive cloud forest on the high plateau. Towering trees are covered with vines, ferns, and moss, forming a dense canopy completely blocking out the sun, with little undergrowth between the trees. Celaque means "box of water" in Lenca; 11 major rivers begin at Celaque, which gives an idea of how wet it can be.

The park covers 266 square kilometers,

PARQUE NACIONAL CELAQUE

with 159 square kilometers in the core zone above 1,800 meters. Although treacherously steep on its flanks, Celaque levels off in a plateau at about 2,500 meters, which is where the true cloud forest begins. You can spend hours or days admiring the 230 species of flora, and quietly keeping an eye out for quetzals, trogons, hawks, or any of the other 269 bird species identified in the park, as well as for the rarer mountain mammals, such as armadillos, raccoons, white-tailed deer, howler monkeys, wild boar, and gray foxes. Patient watchers might catch a glimpse of a quetzal at Celaque, particularly on the lower trails, and during the months of March and April. (Some of the best bird-watching is closer to the visitors center; be sure to bring your binoculars.)

Added bonuses are two well-maintained trails, one leading to the highest peak, which passes a visitors center and two basic encampments on the way, and another to a slightly lower peak, also passing the visitors center and one encampment. This makes Celaque accessible for the casual backpacker who is after a good hike but doesn't want to hire a guide or try to navigate by compass and topographical map.

The more adventuresome hiker should plan for at least one night out, to be sure to have time to spend in the cloud forest, which is only in the highest reaches of the mountain. This would require spending a night at Don Tomás camp, in a very rough, rather nasty hut; better yet, come prepared with your own tent (Hotel Guancascos can help with arrangements for camping gear). Trips up into the forest and, if you're really industrious, all the way to the top and back in one day are possible but exhausting. In fact, the trail beyond Don Tomás camp is pretty steep, best only for those in very good physical shape.

Visitors Center

The Celaque visitors center, some nine kilometers from Gracias at the base of the mountain, is a great place for day visitors. Located at the edge of the forest next to the Río Arcágual, this is a very peaceful spot to relax, and plenty of easy day hiking is possible nearby, along the river. There are restrooms and cold-water showers, as well as a barbecue pit, if you're inspired to lug food and fuel up the mountainside. It is US$2.50 to enter the park, and an additional US$2.50 to stay the night (whether in the visitors center or in your own tent).

To get to the visitors center from Gracias, arrange a ride (US$15) with the guide Marco Aurelio, or through your hotel, to the last gate blocking vehicles from entering the park, from which point the visitors center is another half-hour walk. Or you can start walking from Gracias and hope a pickup truck comes by. It's about a 2.5-hour walk from Gracias to the center by the road, or a bit less by a trail leaving the road just outside Gracias, which follows along a stone wall and rejoins the dirt road to the visitors center near a school.

On the Trail

From the visitors center, it is possible to hike several shorter trails; even a 45-minute walk brings you across creeks and through the forest. A map of the trails from the Hotel Guancascos is not necessary for the main trails, but it's sometimes nice to have along. The trail map from Guancascos is much more useful than the topographical map, which does not show the trails. The topographical maps covering the entire park are *Gracias 2459 I*, *La Campa 2459 II*, *San Marcos de Ocotepeque 2459 III*, and *Corquín 2459 IV*. Otherwise ask the park caretaker for directions.

The trail up Celaque follows the Río Arcágual upstream from the visitors center for a short while, ascends a steep hillside, then parallels the mountain. It continues upward at a less steep grade to **Campamento Don Tomás** at 2,050 meters, about a three-hour walk from the visitors center, where you'll find a tin shack with three rudimentary bunks inside and an outhouse. It's pretty grim accommodations, best avoided if possible. (Not to mention that the shack is sometimes locked, so check with the guard at the visitors center beforehand if you plan on using it.) You might prefer to pitch a tent rather than use the cabin, though it can be a relief to have a roof overhead if it's raining.

Beyond the first camp, the trail heads straight up a steep hillside. This is the hardest stretch of trail, and climbing it often entails clinging to roots and tree trunks to pull yourself up the invariably muddy path. Descending this stretch of trail is particularly treacherous. After 2–3 hours of difficult hiking, the trail reaches **Campamento Naranjo,** nothing more than a couple of flat tent sites and a fire pit on the plateau's edge, at 2,560 meters. As you wipe the sweat and mud off your face as you climb, take a look around at the plants and trees. By the time the trail reaches the plateau, you will have entered the cloud forest.

From Campamento Naranjo, it's another two hours or so to the peak, but it goes up and down over gentle hills instead of straight up. Keep a close eye out for the plastic tags tied to tree branches—the lack of undergrowth in the tall, spacious forest makes it easy to lose track of the trail. The final ascent to the top of **Cerro de las Minas** (2,849 meters) is a half hour of fairly steep uphill climbing, but go slow and listen for the quetzals and trogons that live there. The peak is marked by a wooden cross, and if the clouds haven't moved in, you'll have superb views over the valleys to the east. From the visitors center to the peak is six kilometers and about 1,500 meters in elevation gain.

You could, theoretically, hike all the way

COLOSUCA: THE LEGEND BEHIND THE NAME

Lencan legend has it that a poor widow struck out in the forest in search of food for her 10 children. Finding only a few fruits, she cried out, "Lord, help me, I'm alone and cannot feed my children!" her voice shaking and eyes filled with tears.

A breeze began to blow, creating a whirlwind of leaves. A ray of light broke through the trees, and a loving voice spoke. It was God, whispering in the widow's ear what she needed to do in order to provide for her children, and letting her know that she was not alone.

The next morning, the widow awoke to the sound of her children laughing. She observed the innocent joy of her little ones, the glorious blue sky, and thought, "What I heard couldn't be true! Why would God speak to me? It's better I go out again in search of food for my children...."

Hearing her words, God decided to punish this woman of little faith, and as soon as she reached the forest, a breeze began to blow once more, and a ray of light penetrated the trees, illuminating the woman, whose feet were transformed into talons, and whose arms began to sprout white feathers.

"Noooo!" shouted the widow, until her lips could no longer form a word, but only a whistle. According to the legend, this bird is called the colosuca, which flies over the land to watch over her children.

Today, the word Colosuca has been adopted by the region, particularly to refer to the Lenca towns in Lempira–Gracias, Belén, La Campa, San Marcos de Caiquín, San Manuel Colohete, and San Sebastián–and the Parque Nacional Celaque.

---

from the visitors center to the peak and back in a day, but it would be a tough day, and would leave no time for enjoying the cloud forest. A better plan for a short trip is to spend the night in a tent either at Campamento Don Tomás or higher up at Campamento Naranjo. On your way down, be sure to leave the high plateau not long after midday to ensure that you get back to the visitors center before dark, and hopefully catch a ride into Gracias. If you leave the trail in the high part of the cloud forest, take good care to keep your bearings, as it's very easy to get lost.

Shortly after leaving the visitors center on the way to Campamento Don Tomás, you will see a trail branching off to the left, leading to Cerro El Gallo (2,383 meters), a slightly lower peak. The view from the ridge ranges from incredible to very weird and misty to no view at all, depending on the clouds. After climbing the peak, the trail connects to the main trail just above Campamento Don Tomás. The loop via El Gallo and Don Tomás makes a great, but long, day hike through three different habitats, with occasional clearings from which to admire the view and wildlife. From the visitors center, the round-trip takes 6–8 hours.

It's often cold and always wet (especially in the afternoons), so come prepared with proper clothing, including stiff boots, a waterproof jacket, and a warm change of clothes kept in a plastic bag. Both campsites are next to running water. Many visitors drink the water untreated, as there is no human habitation above, but it's better to treat the water first.

Some camping gear is available for rent at Restaurante Guancascos.

◖ LENCA VILLAGES SOUTH OF GRACIAS

The "Colosuca Community," as defined by Gracias's tourist office, encompasses the hillside villages of La Campa, San Marcos Caiquín, San Manuel Colohete, San Sebastián, and Belén, with the town of Gracias as the hub. All but Belén have beautiful and grandiose colonial churches, vestiges of the influence and religious fervor of Guatemala City in the 1700s. Major efforts have been made to develop community tourism, and there are increasing numbers of activities and amenities for visitors. A trip to La Campa and San Manuel Colohete can easily be made in a day if you have or arrange your own transportation, or adventurous travelers can easily stretch out their time in the region over several days, with plenty of great hiking in the pine-covered hills.

To get to the Lencan villages, there is a daily bus leaving Gracias at 11:30 A.M.), passing through La Campa about an hour later and onward to San Manuel de Colohete and San Sebastián. To get back to Gracias from the villages, there is a single early-morning bus, departing from San Sebastián at 6 A.M., then passing through San Manuel de Colohete (6:30 A.M.), and La Campa (7 A.M.). Belén has its own buses, departing Gracias at 8:30 A.M., 11:30 A.M., 3:10 P.M., and 5:30 P.M., and departing from Belén for Gracias at 7:30 A.M., 9:30 A.M., 1 P.M., and 4 P.M. Because bus times can change, it is wise to double-check locally, or look at the website www.colosuca.com, which includes travel information. For private transportation (and a guide), contact Marco Aurelio Rodriguez (tel. 504/2656-0627 or 9870-8821, guiamarcoslenca@yahoo.com).

La Campa

Sixteen kilometers from Gracias by a fairly well-maintained dirt road is the Lenca village of La Campa, famed in the region for both its earthenware pottery and its annual festival, celebrated February 22–25. Even if you only have a short time to spend in this region, a day trip from Gracias to La Campa is a must, to get an idea of what village life is like in the rural mountains of western Honduras. With only about 400 residents tucked into a small valley, La Campa is one of those supremely calm, quiet, uncomplicated mountain villages where it seems nothing, not even visits from outlandish foreigners, disturbs the rhythm of everyday life.

The **Iglesia de San Matías** in the center of town was begun in 1690, renovated in 1938, and colorfully repainted at the end of 2010. It's a fine example of the churches found in many nearby villages, complete with a carved altarpiece and painted saint statues—although only open during Sunday mass (if you ask around, you may be able to find the groundsman to open it for you). The smaller **La Ermita** church on a hill above town was built in 1890.

During the week leading up to February 22, La Campa transforms from a sleepy village into the bustling site of one of the best-known annual *ferias* in the region. Pilgrims from all over western Honduras and Guatemala flood the town to pay homage to the town's patron saint, San Matías, and participate in the celebrations, which include the traditional *guancascos* exchange of saints with other villages, music, and ritual costume dancing. Watch for the Baile del Garrobo; a *garrobo* is a type of lizard, and the dance *(baile)* recalls when a man followed a lizard to a hole in a tree where an image of San Matías was found.

The canyon and dramatic hillsides behind town can be reached by trail. Several caves reputedly line the riverbank. On the hill behind the church, a trail winds upward, leading to **Cruz Alta** four kilometers away, a good day hike through the forest. This hill has long been venerated by people throughout the region. According to local legend, long ago the valley was struck by a series of earthquakes, which terrified the populace. So strong were the quakes that a new mountain was created. In hopes peace would return, the local priest advised the people to carry crosses and sacred images to the top of the new mountain. When this was accomplished, the quakes ceased, and since then, the hill has been considered sacred. A 30-minute hike takes you up to the **Mirador San Juanera** above town, a great spot for taking panoramic pictures if the day is clear.

La Campa is the renowned center for traditional Lencan pottery, which is brown or red, not black and white like the "Lencan"

Iglesia de San Matías in La Campa, dating from 1690, got a facelift in 2010.

pottery that is sold in most souvenir shops across the country (that black-and-white pottery comes from the region surrounding Nacaome, in southern Honduras). The **Centro de Interpretación de Alfarería Lenca** at the top edge of town is a new museum with good displays of pottery. In three homes around town (each marked by a blue sign with a symbol of a pot), you can watch pottery demonstrations and then have a go yourself. Be forewarned: You will have to wait until the following afternoon to take home your masterpiece. Pottery made by locals is available for sale in the homes that offer demonstrations and in a couple of other shops.

PRACTICALITIES

The **Hostal J.B.** (tel. 504/2625-4737 or 9925-6042, hostal-jb@yahoo.com, US$16 s/d), in a large house one block north from the bottom of the park, has five comfortable rooms with wood furniture, each with private bath. Guests can use the attractive living and dining rooms or hang out in the garden with its spectacular view of the hills. The *hostal* is also home to **Cafetería Lenka,** which serves snacks like *empanadas, baleadas,* tacos, *ticucos* (a type of tamal), and coffee, and will make meals for guests. If the hostal is all booked up, the other option in town is the 16-room **Hotel Vista Hermosa** (tel. 504/2625-4770, US$10.50 s, US$16 d). Rooms are clean and simple with a TV, drinking water is provided for free, and the eponymous beautiful view *(vista hermosa)* is from a small shared balcony where it'd be nice to sit with a beer and relax. There are very basic rooms available on a monthly basis as well; you are expected to bring any furniture you want beyond the bed.

At the entrance to town is **Comedor y Artesanías La Bendición,** another spot to pick up some pottery or a meal.

There is a **Centro Comunitario de Conocimiento y Comunicación** (9 A.M.–9 P.M. Mon.–Fri.) across the small square behind the

Tourist attractions and facilities are well-marked in the Colosuca region.

east over spectacular mountain countryside, past one of Lenca warrior Lempira's old fortresses at Cerro Caraquín, near the village of Guanajulque. The hike is possible in one day or a more relaxed two days, and guides can be found in Caiquín by asking around. You can also make it to the reputedly fine village of Santa Cruz, passing through unusual colored-earth countryside, in about five hours from Caiquín.

The same bus that services La Campa leaves Gracias for San Marcos Caiquín at 12:30 P.M. The return is at 6:30 A.M.

San Manuel de Colohete

From the crest of the last hill on the road from La Campa, the view down over San Manuel is exceptionally lovely. The village sits on a rise above the junction of three rivers pouring off the side of Celaque, which soars skyward in a sheer wall that dwarfs the whitewashed village. With clouds almost perpetually wreathing the hills above town, it feels as though San Manuel has been lost in the mists of time, disconnected from anything save the stunning landscape surrounding it.

Similar in design to La Merced church in Gracias, the plaster, tile-roofed **Iglesia de Nuestra Señora de Concepción** features an ornately sculptured facade, and remnants of centuries-old mud paintings are still visible around the beautifully painted, gold-leafed wooden altar. Not one nail was used in the ceiling, which bears traces of centuries-old floral designs. Locals proudly claim that it's known as "the Sistine Chapel of Latin America," and only the most insensitive won't be entranced by the church's primitive elegance. Out front is a colorful flower garden with benches. Built in 1721, it has an air of decaying beauty, although a restoration plan is underway with financial help from the Spanish government.

municipal building on the south side of the park. There are also public restrooms at the park.

San Marcos Caiquín

West of La Campa, the road to San Manuel Colohete deteriorates. Three kilometers from La Campa, a dirt road turns off, leading another twelve kilometers to Caiquín. A restored colonial church stands in the center of the village, again open only for Sunday mass. Reportedly, the Caiquín church holds some well-preserved paintings on the plaster walls and a fine wooden altar. The folks at **Comedor Daniela** by the church are very friendly, and they can usually help find a bed. Doris who works there can help you find guides nearby also. Grim accommodations are also available at Casa de Angela up the hill. Internet service is available at the municipal **Sala de Computo** next to the *alcaldía* (city hall).

From Caiquín, well-beaten trails head

Comedor Edin, opposite the turnoff to San Sebastián near the entrance to town, has *baleadas* and tacos for a buck apiece, and meals for US$2.25. **Golosinas Conchita**

traditional Lencan pottery

(6:30 A.M.–9 P.M. daily) has a larger menu, including *licuados,* and soup on Sundays, and Conchita will make anything you want (that she knows how to make) if you order in advance so that she can get the ingredients.

Just down the road is **Hotel Emanuel,** with nine simple rooms. Rooms with shared bath cost US$3.60 per person, while the rooms with private baths cost US$16–18 and can sleep up to five people.

Internet is available at the **Centro Comunitario de Conocimientos y Comunicaciones,** facing the park (closed Sun.).

The town's annual *feria* is December 7–8. The 1st and 15th of each month are market days, where you can find wicker crafts and chairs as well as standard market goods.

Don't be surprised if residents of San Manuel or any of these farther-flung villages don't know quite what to make of a foreign visitor, especially if not accompanied by a Honduran. But the worst that will happen is everyone will stare wordlessly at you, and the children will pester you relentlessly, often asking for money to buy junk food. Keep a friendly smile on your face and all will be well.

From the grass square, with the church on your right, look for the trail heading down to the river, for a place to cool off and admire the scenery. Here you can cross over and hike up the far side along trails as high as you'd like, or walk upriver to the *aldea* of San Antonio, where you can be sure they haven't met too many foreigners.

San Manuel is 16 kilometers by very rough dirt road west of La Campa. The bus to Gracias passes through at 6:30 A.M., and from Gracias, the bus to San Manuel departs at 12:45 P.M. The ride takes a little over two hours.

San Sebastián

The dirt road from San Manuel to San Sebastián, another attractive village farther west around Celaque, is not too bad, although there is a deep river crossing (read: You need a 4WD and should not attempt in the rainy season). **Comedor Alicia** on the square has meals (and also a couple of very basic rooms). If no ride is available, walk the road in 3–4 hours, and from there, you can continue walking several more hours on a remnant of the old *camino real* to Belén Gualcho, where you can spend the night and catch a ride the next day to Santa Rosa de Copán. One bus a day runs the 45 kilometers between San Sebastián and Gracias, leaving San Sebastián at 6 A.M., and Gracias at 12:45 P.M.

If you're a hiker, ask locals about "El Alta," which is a nesting site for hawks and eagles.

Belén

Twenty-four kilometers south on the Gracias–La Esperanza road, take a left and go three kilometers to reach the tiny town of Belén. The pavement ends just when you reach the town, whose dirt roads can be severely rutted during the rainy season. Although Belén has joined the Colosuca Tourist Circuit, it is only just beginning to develop any kind of amenities for visitors. There are two churches: 19th-century El Rosario on the main square, and the Ermita de Belén a block away. **Comedor Lourdes** has the standards at cheap prices (US$2.50–3). There are four buses a day between Gracias and Belén (departing Gracias at 8:30 A.M., 11:30 A.M., 3:10 P.M., and 5:30 P.M.; departing Belén at 7:30 A.M., 9:30 A.M., 1 P.M., and 4 P.M.).

SAN JUAN

About halfway up the mountain road between Gracias and La Esperanza, where a side road turns south toward Erandique, is the town of San Juan, set amid fine countryside. In the past, Peace Corps volunteers worked with the community to develop tourist information and amenities for naturalist and cultural experiences in the region. While the network that once was seems to have fallen by the wayside, you may still be able to track down information from Gladys Nolasco, owner of the shop Docucentro Israel, around the corner from Los Jarritos restaurant, for activities such as pottery and coffee roasting demonstrations, horseback tours, and visits to nearby waterfalls.

Accommodations and Food

The newest hotel in town, **Hotel Junior** (tel. 504/9962-2587, US$8 s, US$10.50 d) is also its best. Located right along the highway, the 10 rooms are in a two-story building set behind the family home. There's hot water, and even a showerhead (for those tired of budget hotels with the water coming straight out of a pipe rather than an actual shower!), and the bathrooms are nicely tiled.

There is a simple but attractive cabin in the hills available for tourists, run by Jesús Castillo. If you speak Spanish, you can call Jesús directly at 504/9658-9629; otherwise see if Gladys at Docucentro Israel might be able to help. Jesús will also prepare meals (US$2) and arrange trips, horseback riding, etc., for a charge. Tips are welcome.

There are several *comedores* sprinkled throughout town, and another new addition, **Los Jarritos** (7:30 A.M.–9 P.M. daily), on the main road through town (not the highway, but the town road), serving snacks like tacos and nachos, and burger/fries/soft drink combo meals for US$1.50–3.

Getting There and Away

San Juan is roughly 30 kilometers, or about 50 minutes, from Gracias, on a road that is potholed, but paved. Buses cost US$2 and run hourly between the two cities. Buses from San Juan to La Esperanza cost a little more (about US$2.35), but leave hourly. It takes about an hour to travel the 30 kilometers between San Juan and La Esperanza.

Erandique

At San Juan, about halfway along the road between Gracias and La Esperanza, a rough dirt road turns south 24 kilometers to Erandique,

LEMPIRA: THE MAN IN THE MONEY

The name of Honduras's currency, lempira, honors the country's first great hero, a Lenca warrior who led his people in a war against the Spaniards during the early years of the conquest of Honduras.

Spaniards first penetrated the mountainous region of present-day western Honduras in the early 1530s. From the start, the native Lenca people fiercely resisted the newcomers, and in 1537, Honduran governor Francisco de Montejo led a strong contingent of soldiers into the region and called a meeting of native chiefs. All but one of the chiefs showed up—and were promptly hanged by the Spaniards.

The chief who did not attend the meeting was Lempira ("Lord of the Mountains" in Lenca), described by the Spaniards as about 35-40 years old, "of medium stature, with strong arms, brave, and intelligent." Instead, Lempira gathered a large force of warriors at Peñol de Cerquín and at several other mountain redoubts near what is now Erandique. He convinced the Cares tribe to join the fight, according to legend, by scorning them: "How is it so many brave men in their own land can be subjugated miserably by so few foreigners?"

At the time, the Spaniards did indeed have very few men in Honduras. Just when Montejo thought he had subdued the region, Lempira coordinated surprise attacks on several Spanish settlements from his mountain fortress. In response, the conquistadors assembled a force led by Captain Alonso de Cáceres to take the fortress at Peñol de Cerquín.

Lempira had chosen his spot well. The steep, rugged Peñol did not allow the Spaniards to employ their horses, and they were unable to take the fortress by force. After six months of blockading, the Peñol still had not been taken, as Lenca warriors easily snuck past the Spanish soldiers in the forest and had no trouble keeping themselves provisioned. Other Indian groups, seeing Lempira's success in holding out against the Spaniards, began their own uprisings across the province.

History offers us three different versions of what happened next. According to *Historia de América*, written almost 100 years after the event, the frustrated Cáceres, unable to take the fortress by direct attack or by siege, decided to trick Lempira. Calling on the Lenca chief to discuss peace terms, Cáceres hid a soldier among the Spanish horses. Just as Lempira was disdainfully rejecting any terms short of Spanish withdrawal, the hidden soldier shot and killed the chief with an *arquebus*.

More recently, Honduran and Canadian historians uncovered a document in Spain from the *Audiencia de México*. In the report, dated 1558, Spanish soldier Rodrigo Ruíz states that *he* killed the Lenca leader in combat and took his head back to Siguatepeque as proof of his actions.

Yet another version comes from the Lenca town of Gualcinse. Local tradition has long held that Lempira was indeed shot while listening to a peace proposal by the Spaniards, but that he was only wounded, and his warriors carried him off to hiding. A contingent of Spaniards heard of Lempira's whereabouts, came to the town, killed him on his sickbed, cut off his head, and brought it back to Siguatepeque.

In some manner, Lempira's uprising and death must have been a last gasp for the Lenca; the formerly fierce warriors never again threatened Spanish rule in the region.

Lempira watches over Gracias's central square.

an exceptionally beautiful, rural colonial town set amid the Sierra de las Neblinas. The mountains around Erandique were the old stomping grounds of Lenca warrior Lempira when he waged his guerrilla war against the Spanish conquistadors in the 16th century.

Erandique has three *parques* (squares), each fronted by a small but very fine colonial-era church. Formerly, each of the squares had a massive ceiba tree in front, planted more than a century ago, but now only two survive. One of these remaining two ceibas was nearly split in half when struck by lightning. The one intact tree is impressively huge, dwarfing the square and the church behind it. A large statue to Lempira stands in the center of the main square.

Bemused visitors to Erandique may find themselves surrounded by men, women, and children asking if they would like to buy opals. As it turns out, the surrounding countryside is one of the most famous areas in the Americas for the precious stone. Several different grades of opals are mined nearby, including black, white, river, garden, rainbow, milk, and the valuable aurora opals. Honduran opals are considered particularly valuable because of the frequent presence of scarlet coloring. Local campesinos are also always turning up obsidian arrowheads and other objects from pre-Columbian and conquest times and often trying to sell them to visitors for very little money.

Apart from the occasional opal-buyer, Erandique doesn't receive many foreign visitors, so you may be the recipient of a few curious but usually good-natured stares from town residents. Anyone with a modicum of openness and minimal Spanish will quickly find the friendly townsfolk ready to chat about the town or the world at large. The town's annual festival is held on January 20 in honor of San Sebastián, and holidays for San Antonio (June 13), Lempira (July 20), and the Virgen de La Merced (September 8) are also observed. Gladys Nolasco in San Juan also has information on tourist activities in Erandique.

Reportedly, **Hotel Steven** (Barrio Gualmaca, US$5.50 s, US$8 d) has comfortable rooms, hot showers, and cable TV. There are a couple of basic *comedores* with standard *típico* food. There are also a couple of Internet cafés (domestic and international calls can be made from the one near the central park), a gas station, and a small medical clinic.

One minibus runs between Gracias and Erandique daily, leaving Erandique early in the morning for the 2.5-hour, US$2 trip. Another bus leaves at 5 A.M. for the 4-hour trip to La Esperanza, US$2.50. Finding a *jalón* on one of the regularly passing pickup trucks is frequently possible.

Near Erandique

The pine-forested mountains around Erandique are excellent for hiking, with footpaths leading in all directions. For a short afternoon trip, ask the way to **Las Cuatro Chorreras,** a wide waterfall about a half-hour walk south of town down the valley.

Those with an interest in history, or looking for a good long walk, may want to make a pilgrimage to **Peñol de Cerquín,** Lempira's unconquered fortress in his war against the Spanish. Ask a local for directions to the path leaving Erandique up the southeast flank of Montaña Azacualpa to **San Antonio Montaña,** a collection of huts and a small primary school perched on the side of the mountain. The trail rounds the side of the mountain near the schoolhouse, and from that spot, the rocky spire of the Peñol can be seen in the valley below. From the schoolhouse, a trail continues down the mountain to the Peñol, or you can continue up the trail on the far side of Azacualpa, which eventually connects to the Erandique–Mapulaca road. This round-trip can be done easily in a day, with plenty of time to admire the views, but a trip to the Peñol would probably require one night of camping.

Other nearby mountains, such as

Coyucatena, Congolón, and Piedra Parada (according to local lore, the site of Lempira's assassination), can also be hiked up—generally, trails lead in all directions. Reportedly, a monument to Lempira sits atop Cerro Congolón, and vestiges of indigenous fortresses are found on Coyucatena. From Erandique, you could walk northwest to Celaque and Gracias in a couple of days, if equipped with good maps and a compass or a local guide. Camping is safe, but it's always best to check with a local campesino before pitching a tent. Guides for this region can usually be found in San Juan, and Max Elvir of Lenca Travel in Santa Rosa de Copán also offers tours in the area.

San Francisco de Lempira, 28 kilometers from Erandique (hitchhiking very possible), is a lovely little village, with electric power supplied by solar panels from a UNESCO project. About three kilometers from town is a cave with a number of interesting prehistoric paintings of animals, hands, and one dancing human figure. Ask in San Francisco for someone to show you the way.

South Toward El Salvador

The road leaving Erandique to the south heads up over the mountain behind town and continues on to Mapulaca near the Salvadoran border. Little traffic passes on this road even in the dry season, but hitchhiking is possible if you're patient. It might be quicker to find a guide and walk by trails through the lovely countryside. From Mapulaca, a dirt road winds its way north via Valladolid and Tomalá to La Labor, where it meets the Nueva Ocotepeque–Santa Rosa de Copán highway. This is serious adventure-travel country—pickup trucks and hiking are the only means of transport all the way. Don't plan on getting anywhere quickly. A couple of veteran Honduran travelers report that this is one of their favorite parts of the country, with friendly folk and spectacular scenery, as well as horrifically bad dirt roads. Decent hostels and basic food are available in both Tomalá and Mapulaca, and probably elsewhere too if you ask around.

LA ESPERANZA

The capital of the Intibucá department, La Esperanza lies in the heart of the most traditional Lenca region in the country. It is a twin city with Intibucá (yes, there is a city with the same name as the department), the two located

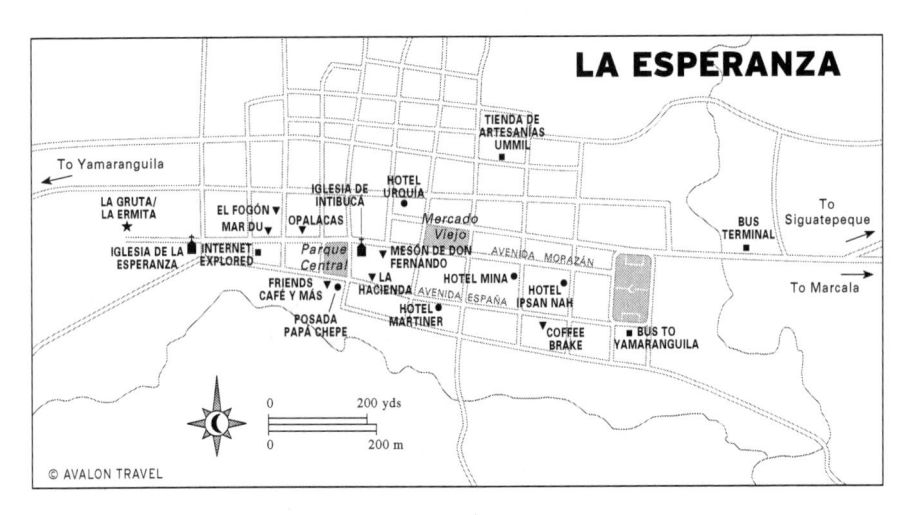

Lencan women attend mass at the Catholic church of Intibucá, the twin city of La Esperanza.

so close together that they form a single chunk of urbanity. They share the central park, but each has its own Catholic church. Together they have a population of about 40,000, and the market area often swarms with residents from surrounding villages coming in to trade their produce or buy goods. It's especially lively on weekend mornings, when you can watch Lenca women wearing colorful dresses and head scarves going about their business. Local handicrafts can be found in a few shops, most notably the cooperative **Tienda de Artesanías UMMIL** (7:30 A.M.–4:30 P.M. Mon.–Sat., 7:30 A.M.–noon Sun.), with fruit wines, pottery, pine needle baskets, and the like, all made by Lencan women.

Set in a mountain valley surrounded by pine forest in the heart of the Sierra de Opalaca at 1,980 meters, La Esperanza is Honduras's highest city. The climate is cool, with daytime temperatures normally hovering between 10 and 20°C (50–68°F). Originally, the Lenca village of Eramaní, which means "Land of Pottery" in Lenca, La Villa de La Esperanza was officially founded on September 23, 1848. The Spanish name derives, according to local legend, from a priest who came to the area with his younger cousin during colonial times to convert the Lenca. The young cousin became enamored with a local girl and fathered a child with her. The priest promptly sent his cousin away in anger, but the girl and her child never gave up hope *(esperanza)* that the young Spaniard would return.

Sights and Events

As in many colonial towns, the churches are the main sights within the city limits. The church on the town square is the **Iglesia de Intibucá,** unusual in that although the nicer church, it was the one that traditionally served the indigenous people. The Catholic church of La Esperanza is at the edge of town near the exit to Yamaranguila and Gracias, and is a somewhat simpler affair. Just above, on a hill overlooking town, is **La Gruta,** the cave, with a small chapel inside known as **La Ermita,** which is the site of religious services during Semana Santa and other special occasions. The main street running past the square turns into a stairway, reputedly built in the 1930s by recruits from the local prison, which leads up to the cave.

The **Festival Gastronómico del Choro y el Vino** celebrates the local wild mushrooms and fruit wines (two regional specialties) on the last weekend in June (or sometimes the first weekend of July) each year. A potato festival is celebrated in late July (or sometimes at the beginning of August), and a Lencan crafts fair is held in December.

Accommodations
UNDER US$25
The best budget hotel option in town is the new **Hotel Martiner** (tel. 504/2783-0931,

martiner10@yahoo.com, US$10.50 s, US$16 d). Yes, it's basic, but good for a basic hotel; the rooms are big enough and very clean, with decent sheets, hot water, and TVs. There is a nice rooftop with a hammock, chairs, and table where guests can hang out, as well as a small cafeteria where guests can order *comida típica* for breakfast or dinner. No wireless Internet, but there is a connection via modem that guests can use. There are plans to open a small cafeteria for guests on the rooftop.

If the Martiner is full, the rooms on the second floor of **Hotel Urquía** (two blocks north of the church, 504/2774-3955, US$8 s, US$16 d) are acceptable. They have been recently repainted; hopefully they'll get some new sheets soon too. Don't bother to even look at the rooms with a shared bath, they're hideous. Those on their last lempira can head to **Hotel Venezia** (tel. 504/2783-1424, US$5.25 s, US$8 d with shared bath, US$10 s, US$15 d with private bath). Did the owners read our past criticism about dingy rooms? Because now they're brightly painted red and blue. It's an improvement. The rooms with private bath are acceptable, even though there's just a curtain between you and the toilet; the shared baths are still depressing. But cheap.

Stepping up a notch in price is **Hotel Las Margaritas** (tel. 504/2783-1066, hlasmargaritas@hotmail.com, US$18.50 s, US$29 d). The 15 rooms have cheery bedspreads and *electroduchas* for hot water showers. The main difference between here and Hotel Martiner is that Las Margaritas has wireless Internet throughout the hotel.

Out near the highway to Siguatepeque is **Hotel Molino Real** (tel. 504/2783-4067, hotelmolinorealhn@hotmail.com, US$18.50 s, US$ 31.50 d). Rooms have cable TV and tiled bathrooms, there is wireless Internet throughout the hotel, there are plans to put a restaurant, staff is friendly, and the price for a single room is especially good. The drawback: the cement-block walls feel rather dreary, despite being painted in cheery colors.

US$25-50

A example of hospitality gone right, the new **◖ Posada Papá Chepe** (tel. 504/2783-0443, posadapapachepe@gmail.com, US$29 s, US$34 d), is a newly renovated colonial house situated on the corner of the town square, converted into a small hotel. Rooms have wood ceilings and terra-cotta tile floors, wireless Internet, TVs, and carved wood furniture. There is a small but lush interior garden and plans for a second-floor library-slash-bar. Our only concern: Will the rooms under the bar be able to hear every step taken above? There is a good selection of handicrafts and other souvenirs in the hotel reception.

The motel-style **Hotel Mina** (tel. 504/2783-1071, US$29 s US$31.60 d) is a reasonable deal, with spacious newer rooms that aspire to elegance and smaller, older rooms for five bucks less. Semi-suites with two double beds and a small sitting area are also available for US$37. There have been reports of insufficiently clean bathrooms; you may want to check yours before putting any money down. On the next block is **Hotel La Esperanza** (tel. 504/2783-0068, luispalencia04@yahoo.com, US$21 s, US$26 d, suite US$37 s/d), with some worn rooms and other newer ones (the worn ones being the cheaper ones, naturally). In addition to being newer, the suites have a king bed plus a double, a couch, a large plasma TV, and a coffeemaker (as well as slightly tacky mismatched linens on the beds). There is wireless Internet throughout the hotel's 35 rooms, and a restaurant is on-site.

Around the corner and a touch more drab (although with some sunnier newer rooms and wireless Internet) is the four-story **Hotel Ipsan Nah** (tel. 504/2783-2086, hotelipsan-nah@yahoo.com, US$34 s, US$41 d). The newer rooms have a little balcony, a desk, a fridge, even a fresh flower in a vase. Some rooms, but not all, have a fan—although it's not needed

La Esperanza's town pharmacy is housed in a building from 1885.

much of the year in chilly La Esperanza. The chicken (US$4–6.25) is popular at the Ipsan Nah's restaurant. These three hotels can often be full, so be sure to book in advance if you have a preference.

There are three nice sets of cabins outside of town, popular with weekenders from Tegucigalpa. Our favorite is the highly regarded and family-run **Casa del Arroyo B&B** (tel. 504/2717-7161, www.casadelarroyohn.com, US$40–50 s, US$11–13 each additional person, discounts for children). The five rooms are in adobe and log cabins around a countryside property, and can sleep from 2–8 people, all have TVs, some have DVD players, and one has a fridge. Two of the rooms also have a kitchen, which can be used for an additional cost of US$11. There is a kids play area and a common area that guests can use, and dinner can be arranged upon request. Tours are offered to nearby attractions (Chiligatoro Lagoon, the Río Grande waterfall, Cerro de Hoyos, Valle de Azacualpa, and the looms of El Cacao for first-time guests) for US$40 for up to four people. Tours to Gracias and the nearby villages are possible as well. Be sure to either check the map on their website, or call to arrange a meeting point, as the hotel isn't totally easy to find.

Cabañas Los Pinos (tel. 504/2783-2034, www.lospinosresort.com, US$30.50 s, US$12 each additional person in standard rooms, or in wood or stone cabins; US$43 s, US$19 each additional person in cabins with chimney) is a quirky, artistic development a couple of kilometers down the road to Siguatepeque, with a good if slow restaurant and some children's play equipment. The rooms have attractive wooden furniture, and some have sleeping lofts; there is a bit of forest on the property for wandering in, and hammocks in a gazebo for relaxing. There is also an unheated swimming pool, which, given the cool weather in La Esperanza, doesn't see much use.

US$50 AND UP

Cabañas Llanos de la Virgen (tel. 504/2783-0443, US$53 s/d) has attractive, colorfully painted cabins in a countryside setting, each with a full kitchen, dining area, and living room—bring what you want to prepare for breakfast, because there isn't any restaurant on-site. Visitors can wander through the pine forest or read a book in one of the Adirondack chairs on the cabin porches, and there is a basketball court and children's play equipment to keep the little ones busy.

Food

Choros, a type of wild mushroom similar to oyster mushrooms, are the local specialty, although they are only seasonally available at most restaurants. When they're in season, many restaurants offer chicken, beef, and pork dishes with *choros*.

One of the best restaurants in town is ◖ **La Hacienda** (tel. 504/2783-0244, 9 A.M.–10 P.M. daily), with colorful dining rooms decorated with antiques, hides, gourds, and Lencan pottery, and an open-air dining area as well. Grilled meats are the specialties, there are seven varieties of *plato típico* (US$5.25), as well as burgers, tacos, *pinchos* (meat on a skewer), shrimp, fish, fajitas, and more (US$6–8.50 most mains). La Hacienda is one of the few restaurant to offer La Esperanza's famed mushrooms year-round (do they dry them? freeze them?) and in a variety of preparations—soup, sautéed, with chicken, as a sauce on beef (US$5–8). "Intibucan wine" is also offered by the glass here, if you were curious to try one of the local fruit wines but hesitant to buy an entire bottle.

Half a block west of the park is the popular **Restaurante Opalacas** (tel. 504/2783-0503, 10 A.M.–9:30 P.M. daily), specializing in meats served fajita-style on a sizzling hot plate *(a la plancha)*. *Lomo a la plancha con salsa de hongos*, a thin steak served with a sauce of the famous *choros*, is a house specialty. Portions are generous, and there is some children's play equipment inside the restaurant for anyone who might get restless during the longish wait for the food. Burgers and sandwiches are around US$5, while chicken, beef, and fish mains run US$6–10.50.

A block east of the park is **Mesón de Don Fernando** (10 A.M.–10 P.M. daily), located in a renovated house. There is a *menu económico* with items like fajitas and chicken for US$4.75, tilapia and cod dishes in your choice of sauce (garlic, ginger, parmesan, and others) for US$11, and beef entrées for US$10.50–12.50.

If you are looking to eat on the cheap, there are some inexpensive *comedores* by the Hotel Ipsan Nah.

With live music and dancing on Friday and Saturday (8 P.M.–12:45 A.M., the restaurant **El Fogón** (9 A.M.–10 P.M. Tues.–Thurs., until 12:45 A.M. Fri. and Sat.) may be your best bet for entertainment. Kitsch decor covers the walls: sports in one corner, a pirate motif in another. Food ranges from US$4–9, and includes steak with *choros*; the gut-busting *el indito comelón* with sausage, beef, roast chicken, beans, salad, and tortillas; bull testicles; and a sprinkling of Mexican dishes.

Coffee and Snacks

Pretty unique for small-town Honduras is **Mar Du** (9 A.M.–9:30 P.M. Mon.–Sat., 10 A.M.–9:30 P.M. Sun.), a hipster-style coffee shop with comfy couches, espresso drinks, and wine by the glass. Sandwiches and cake by the slice are available, as well as some art, jewelry, and other handicrafts.

At the other end of town is **Coffee Brake**, a funky little shop with coffee drinks and Internet.

Information and Services

Banco Atlántida will change dollars and travelers checks, and provide an advance on a Visa card. MoneyGrams can be received here.

Hondutel and **Honducor** are next to each other on the western edge of the square. There are Internet shops all over town, many offering domestic and international calls as well; one is **Internet Explored** (7 A.M.–10 P.M.

Thurs.–Tues., opening an hour later on Wed.), with Internet for US$0.60 per hour.

If you need help with transportation or otherwise organizing your exploration of the area, **Asingtur** (tel. 504/2783-3931 or 3301-9792, marielaroa80@yahoo.com) is a local tour company that can arrange excursions to the Chiligatoro Lagoon, Río Grande waterfall, or the Valle de Azacualpa.

Getting There and Away

La Esperanza is connected by a well-maintained, 67-kilometer paved road to Siguatepeque. The road heads down out of the mountains, across the Río Otoro valley, past the town of Jesús de Otoro, and back up into the mountains to the junction with the San Pedro Sula–Tegucigalpa highway.

Buses to Siguatepeque leave roughly every hour from the terminal on the edge of town until 4 P.M., charging US$3 for the 90-minute ride. These buses are legendary for being so slow that, according to one laconic local, they will stop on the side of the road even if a chicken appears to wave its wing in the air. If you find a *directo*, pay the extra cents and take it. Buses to Marcala leave from here too, and charge US$2.10 for the hour ride. The road is paved part of the way, and unpaved and terribly rutted the other part (if you're driving, you'll need a 4WD).

Buses to Tegucigalpa and San Pedro Sula with **Carolina** (tel. 504/9945-9240) leave the terminal 11 times daily between 4 A.M. and 3 P.M. Both take about four hours and charge about US$6. **Esperanzano** (tel. 504/9945-9240) runs hourly buses between Tegucigalpa and La Esperanza between 5 A.M. and 5 P.M. (US$6). In Tegucigalpa, the Esperanzano terminal is between 6 and 7 Avenida, one block above Transporte El Rey.

A 75-kilometer road connects La Esperanza to Gracias; it is years into the paving process, with the majority now paved and the dirt portion usually well maintained. The road passes through some lovely high-mountain country. One minibus drives to Gracias each day, leaving at a variable hour in the morning, charging US$4 for the 2.5-hour ride. If you miss that bus, take one of the hourly minivans to San Juan, where you can transfer to the hourly minivan San Juan–Gracias. Finding a ride in the back of a pickup is also easy and safe. Get out to the junction early, and expect to pay a few lempiras for the ride. Leaving from Gracias, head to the bus stop at the eastern edge of town.

South of La Esperanza, dirt roads continue to the villages of Santa Lucía (87 kilometers) and San Antonio (93 kilometers), in the hotter canyon country near the border with El Salvador.

Getting Around

A taxi just about anywhere in town should run US$0.80.

Near La Esperanza

Seven kilometers from La Esperanza is one of the most traditional Lenca communities in the country, **Yamaranguila.** Although they don't see a lot of tourists, residents are accustomed to outsiders, as a Peace Corps agricultural training center is nearby. On certain holidays, traditional dances like the *guancascos* can be seen, though it's hard to find out when and where the dance will be held. You could try asking the local *alcalde* (mayor) for more information on the festivals. Near Yamaranguila is an impressive waterfall, reached by footpath—just ask for directions to **La Chorrera.** Yamaranguila can easily be reached by frequent buses from La Esperanza (US$0.60), which depart from a lot one block east of the Hotel Ipsan Nah.

On the dirt road heading to San Francisco de Opalaca, 11 kilometers from La Esperanza, is **Laguna Chiligatoro,** a picturesque spot to relax and go for a ride in a rowboat, available for rental at the lake. There is a simple restaurant and a nature trail in the surrounding pine forest.

Ten minutes down the road to San Juan and

GUANCASCOS: PEACE CEREMONIES OF THE WESTERN HIGHLANDS

The language and many of the traditions of the Lenca have been lost over the past four and a half centuries. One Lenca ritual still celebrated on certain days in the southern and western highlands is the *guancascos*, a bilateral ceremony between two towns, often neighboring. The *guancascos* is a sort of peace ritual, marking the friendship between the two communities. Many *guancascos* are thought to commemorate a past agreement over the division of farming land or hunting grounds. In the colonial era, and up to the present day in more remote areas, the *guancascos* is the single most important event of the year, marking the time when new village leaders take office and a day of many weddings and baptisms. Although originally a pre-Columbian ritual, since colonial times the *guancascos* has incorporated elements of Catholicism, particularly the use of saints, in the ritual exchange between the communities.

The specific dances and format of the *guancascos* varies widely from town to town, but the general outlines are usually similar. In the days running up to the principal celebration, the townsfolk hold several preliminary ceremonies, such as the Traída de la Pólvora, the bringing of the gunpowder, when the all-important fireworks bought with communal money are brought into the village and divided up among the *mayordomos* (neighborhood leaders). In certain towns, locals hold the Danza de las Escobas, the Broom Dance, so named because the newly elected village leader hands a flowered broom to the previous leader and in return receives La Vara Alta, the Tall Staff. In colonial times, the staff marked the individual responsible for mediating between the community and the Spanish authorities.

On the "big day" of the *guancascos*, festivities begin with the townsfolk parading their patron saint through the streets and then out of town to a designated spot, where the procession meets a second parade from the partner community. Lengthy greetings ensue, punctuated with much fireworks and music, and the two saint icons are exchanged. The two groups then walk together to the church of the main town, which has been decorated with pine branches and filled with copal incense smoke. Representatives of both towns give special speeches in the church, followed by a party of dancing and drinking.

Formerly, the culminating dance of the *guancascos* in many towns was the Danza del Gorrobo, or Dance of the Black Iguana, performed with elaborate costumes, and with musical accompaniment provided by the *chirimía*, a type of flute; *caramba*, a stringed bow; and *sacabuche*, a gourd drum. This dance is no longer widespread–these days, the processions and saint exchange continue, but the elaborate dances have devolved into more unstructured parties.

Although the *guancascos* are meant to be celebrated on certain days, the chosen day seems a bit flexible, and the festival may not be held at all in certain years, depending in large part on whether the townsfolk have enough money for the festivities or not. In a way, it works out perfectly, as the only foreigners who ever get to the festivals are the rare ones who hang out in these villages and get to know the inhabitants, and thus find out. And all in all, those are the sorts of folks who should witness these ceremonies, rather than the video camera-toting package-tour crowd. Almost all *guancascos* are held in January and February, during the dry season, but beyond that, you just have to head to the hills and start asking around.

Gracias is the turnoff for the public baths at **Quiscamote**, a Lencan tradition dating from 1902. The water is cold, but clean, and the installations are surprisingly nice.

The 120-meter waterfall at **Río Grande** is another place where you can easily while away a day. Buses regularly travel between La Esperanza and Río Grande.

There are four supposedly protected natural areas in Intibucá: Montaña Opalaca, Mixcure, Montecillos, and Montaña Verde. Unfortunately, much of the forests have already been severely logged, leaving little of the original flora and fauna intact. Because of its isolated location, only **Refugio de Vida Silvestre Montaña Verde** is still worth visiting, but getting into the forest is no easy task. Located near the border of the Lempira department, in the San Francisco de Opalaca municipality, Montaña Verde can be reached by first getting a bus or *jalón* from La Esperanza to the village of Monte Verde, where a guide can be hired to explore the mountain. As yet, no trails exist, and facilities are limited, but the forest is reputed to be very beautiful and intact. Topographical maps covering the reserve are 1:50,000 *La Iguala 2559 IV* and *La Unión 2560 III*.

For those with an exploratory inclination, the high, pine-forested hill country around La Esperanza provides lovely hiking and mountain biking and is generally considered to be quite safe. A nearby "dwarf forest" is touted as a tourist attraction, but is worth visiting only for the most devout bonsai nut.

A special market called **Mercado Hijas de Intibucá** is held 7 A.M.–4 P.M. Friday–Sunday, in the village of Maracía, a few kilometers outside of La Esperanza on the highway to Siguatepeque. Homegrown fruits and vegetables, plants, and homemade foods are brought and sold by Lencan women from the surrounding area, to sell in what is surely one of the cleanest markets in all of Honduras.

If the weather is warm and you have kids in tow, the **Aqua Park El Molino** (tel. 504/2783-1411, 8 A.M.–6 P.M. daily) is at kilometer 37 on the highway La Esperanza–Jesús de Otoro. There are three pools, a restaurant, and swimsuits available for rent if you've forgotten yours.

From La Esperanza to El Salvador

South of La Esperanza, a dirt highway (in good condition only during the Jan.–May dry season) descends an escarpment down into the hotter lowlands near the Salvadoran border. Beginning from around the area of **San Marcos de Sierra**, on a clear day one can see the volcanoes of San Vicente and San Miguel across the border in El Salvador. The road continues down into a small valley, in the middle of which is the town of **Concepción**, and then continues up again briefly. Beyond Concepción, the road forks three ways: the southeasterly road going through **Colomancagua**, the southern road through **Santa Lucía**, and the southwesterly road through **San Antonio**. All eventually go into El Salvador, but the road through Colomancagua is in the best condition. It first passes through the border crossing of San Fernando, with (at last report) a Honduran border guard who is happy to stamp your passport, but nobody on the Salvadoran side. Continue to the first major Salvadoran town, **Perquín**, where there is an interesting museum about the civil war. From Perquín, the road is paved farther into El Salvador, but be aware that you may have to pay a small fine if you leave El Salvador through a different border, because you don't have an entry stamp. Returning through the same border is no problem. The travelers who've made the trip rate it as well worth it for the adventure of crossing a remote border, with fine views over the countryside.

Ocotepeque

A scruffy border town, Ocotepeque is blessed with a fine setting amid the beautiful mountains at the junction of Honduras, Guatemala, and El Salvador. The town's name derives from the words *ocote*, a local pine tree, and *tepec*, meaning hill. Most travelers who enter here get on the first bus heading in whatever direction they're going, but the hiking aficionado may want to dawdle for a couple of days to see the nearby **Reserva Biológica El Güisayote**, on the crest of the mountains rising right behind town, or **Parque Nacional Trifinio-Montecristo**, which forms the border of the three countries. It's also possible and safe to meander up any of the trails winding into the surrounding hills for a short hike (although it's best not to go alone).

Ocotepeque is divided into "nueva" (new) and "antigua" (old) by a river. In fact, the town is often referred to as "Nueva Ocotepeque," but the designation of new was officially abolished in 1958 (making it harder, of course, to distinguish between the city and the department of the same name). Of note in Antigua Ocotepeque is the colonial church of San Andrés; its traditional dance of "the Moors and the Christians," performed every first of November, is renowned. The dance has been described as one of the most deeply rooted traditions of Honduras—although it is clearly an import from the Spanish *conquistadores*, as it remembers the fight Christians in Spain put up against the invading Arabs (Moors). Beyond that, there's just a few duty-free stores.

ACCOMMODATIONS

Of the several low-priced hotels in town, **Hotel Turista** (tel. 504/2653-3639, US$10.50 s, US$23.50 d with cold water; US$13 s, US$26 d with hot water) is a good value, with clean and spacious rooms with different prices and amenities. The hotel is in Barrio San José, one block east of the highway.

The best in town is probably **Hotel Sandoval** (Bulevar Bo. San Jose and Av. Carlos M. Arita Palomo, tel. 504/2653-3098, www.hotelsandoval.com, US$27 s, US$36 d, including breakfast; rooms with a/c are US$3.70 more). The hotel has a pool, and its restaurant, open daily 7 A.M.–9 P.M., has good food.

Two blocks up from the bus station is the **Hotel Maya Chortis** (tel. 504/2653-2105, US$21 s, US$30 d with fan). All rooms have cable TV and fans, and some have small refrigerators and air-conditioning for just US$4 more. All rooms are supposed to have hot water as well, but guests have reported otherwise. The restaurant, **Don Chepe** (7 A.M.–9 P.M.), has very good meals for US$6–10, and the staff speaks some English. A good value all in all. Parking is available.

Hotel Internacional (Calle Internacional between 1 and 2 Av., tel. 504/2653-2357, hotelinternacional56@yahoo.es, US$21 s, US$30.50 d with fan, a few dollars more for a/c) is a large hotel at the corner of the *parque central*. Rooms have TVs, wireless Internet, and "semi-orthopedic" beds. Breakfast is included in the rate.

FOOD

A number of cheap *comedores* serve up good *plato típico*, eggs, chicken-and-rice plates, and other dishes. One recommended joint is **Comedor San Marino**, on the main highway that runs through town and across the street from the Congolón bus station. It has great *carne asada* (much better than a lot of the *carne asada* in Honduras), chicken, and chorizo. All meals come with beans, toasted tortillas, fried plantains, cheese, sometimes avocado, and *chismol*, a condiment made of chopped tomato, bell pepper, onion, and cilantro. A dinner plate plus a drink is about $3.80. It's delicious.

There are also plenty of places to get *baleadas*. The local favorite is the restaurant across the street from the Liberal Party headquarters. **Hondutel** is across from the Hotel Sandoval, open daily 7 A.M.–9 P.M., while **Honducor** is near the square. For Internet access, try **CiberCafé,** around the corner from Hotel Internacional, on the same street as the police station (US$1/hour), or head to the library, where you can use Internet for free 2–3 P.M. Monday–Friday.

INFORMATION AND SERVICES

Banco de Occidente exchanges dollars and travelers checks, but changing Salvadoran colones or Guatemalan quetzales is best done with money changers at the border, who are usually reliable. There are also money changers right across the street from the Transporte San José office. Everyone in town knows where they are, and they also tend to ask foreign-looking people who are walking by if they want to change money. There also is an ATM in town right next to Banco de Occidente. **Banco Atlántida** can also give a cash advance on a Visa card, and will change dollars to lempiras.

There is a bilingual school, **My Little Red House** (www.mylittleredhouse.weebly.com), that is always looking for **volunteers.** They will accept volunteers for as little as one week, they welcome groups and mission teams, and while teaching experience is always welcome, nothing more than native English-speaking skills are required. Accommodation is provided to volunteers who stay six months or longer. For more information on volunteering, contact Ana Penman at 504/2653-3042.

GETTING THERE AND AWAY

From Ocotepeque, you can catch any of the frequent Sultana, Toritos y Copánecos (tel. 504/2653-3405), Transporte San José, or Congolón (tel. 504/9858-3226) buses coming from the Guatemalan border at Agua Caliente onward to San Pedro Sula for US$8.50–9.50. There are also three direct buses daily (at varying times) to San Pedro Sula from Nueva Ocotepeque.

Buses depart every hour or two between Ocotepeque and Santa Rosa, charging US$4.20 for the 2.5-hour ride, until 3 P.M. Sultana (tel. 504/2662-0940) tends to stop the least, getting to Santa Rosa in a fairly reliable two hours instead of three.

Buses to the border at Agua Caliente cost US$1.50 and run about every half hour until 6 P.M. You can also get to either of the borders, Agua Caliente for Guatemala or El Poy for El Salvador, by taxi. To El Poy by *colectivo* taxi is just US$0.85, or US$5–6 for a private taxi. On the way you will pass El Soldado, a statue on the left side if heading toward the border, commemorating the 1969 war with El Salvador. There are also minibuses, *rapiditos,* that leave for El Poy every 20 minutes from Transportes San José, for US$0.65. Although the border at El Poy is safer than Agua Caliente, it's still much better to pass through both during the day.

Agua Caliente at the Guatemalan Border

Regular buses depart Ocotepeque all day to the Guatemalan border at Agua Caliente (22 kilometers, US$1.50). Between the Honduran and Guatemalan border posts is about three kilometers of lonely road—rides are infrequent, so make sure to get to the border by midafternoon at the latest. Travelers arriving from Esquipulas, Guatemala, will find frequent transportation to Ocotepeque until 6 P.M. daily. The border reportedly closes at 2 A.M., but it's best to get there earlier. Taxis from Ocotepeque charge US$10 (less if you share) and usually go until about 10 P.M. Money changers arrive at 9 A.M.; some offer decent rates, while others are happy to rip you off if you don't know the rates. Beware.

At least six buses daily between 5 A.M. and 6 P.M. drive from the border to San Pedro Sula in six hours (US$7), with stops at Ocotepeque and Santa Rosa de Copán, with Toritos y

Copánecos or Empresa Congolón. Toritos y Copánecos also runs several buses a day directly to Tegucigalpa, nine hours.

El Poy at the Salvadoran Border

Buses run frequently between Ocotepeque and El Poy at the Salvadoran border (seven kilometers, US$0.50) until 7 P.M., but consider taking a collective taxi since it's just US$0.85. Private taxis are about US$6. It's always best to get to the border early to ensure buses onward. The border itself, not much more than a roadside collection of buildings with a lot of semitrucks lined up waiting to cross, is open 6 A.M.–7 P.M. daily.

Exit and Entry Fees

There are sometimes exit fees randomly applied at both borders, typically US$3–5. There shouldn't actually be an exit fee, but Honduras does have a US$3 reentry fee for those from outside of Central America.

NEAR OCOTEPEQUE
Reserva Biológica El Güisayote

The Güisayote reserve is what you would call a last-ditch effort to save a patch of disappearing cloud forest. The reserve covers a ridge above Ocotepeque, and the remaining strip of forest looks for the world like a mohawk haircut, surrounded by denuded hillsides.

It may not be anything like Celaque or some of Honduras's other mountain reserves, but Güisayote has a number of endangered birds and mammals hanging on in the reserve, including quetzals, blue foxes, wild hogs, monkeys, and maybe even a couple of pumas. The views across three countries on a clear day (admittedly rare) and easy access to a cloud forest are enough to make it worth a day trip from Ocotepeque if you travel this way, easily accomplished with or without a private vehicle.

One of the reasons the forest is so decimated is that the Honduran Army built a road along the ridge at the time of the 1969 war with El Salvador in order to patrol the frontier, which gave farmers and ranchers easy access into the hills. That same road is now being allowed by environmental authorities to deteriorate into a trail, which can be used by hikers in the reserve.

To get to Güisayote, take any Santa Rosa–bound bus from Ocotepeque 18 kilometers uphill to El Portillo (The Pass)—at 2,000 meters, this is the highest point of any paved road in Honduras. El Portillo is a collection of huts at the pass, from which a dirt road turns south up into the hills, following the ridge to a Hondutel tower five kilometers from the highway, inside the reserve. A 45-minute walk past the Hondutel tower, the road comes to a three-way junction. The left road turns into a path descending the hillside, while the middle and right-hand paths (formerly dirt roads) continue into the forest. The middle road continues around the mountain to the villages of Ocotlán and Plan de Rancho, from which one can catch a truck ride back to Nueva Ocotepeque. The right-hand branch leads to Cerro El Sillón (Big Chair Mountain), the massive wall behind Ocotepeque. At 2,310 meters, it's the highest peak in the vicinity. Even if you don't go that far, walking along these trails, with forays along animal and hunters' paths deeper into the forest, is an easy way to get a taste of the cloud forest without having to camp out. Wildlife is not extensive, but the patient and quiet can spot a variety of cloud forest birds.

Those visiting the park by car can drive up the entrance road as far as the junction and from there must walk, as the road deteriorates beyond that point.

In the southern section of the reserve is a large mountain lake called Laguna Verde; ask a local campesino to guide you there. North of El Portillo, on the other side of the highway, another dirt road follows the ridge through another, smaller patch of forest.

The reserve extends north onward from the Ocotepeque–Santa Rosa highway and has a good-sized patch of cloud forest, but it is more difficult to reach than the south side, as no roads or major trails head in this direction.

The topographical map covering Güisayote is *Nueva Ocotepeque 2359 II*. Some limited information on the reserve can be found at the Plan Trifinio office (tel. 504/2653-3009) in Ocotepeque, on the edge of town on the road toward El Salvador. Guides are reportedly available into the reserve from the village of San Marcos.

Parque Nacional Trifinio-Montecristo

This national park, jointly administered by Honduras, Guatemala, and El Salvador, comprises a cloud-forested mountain peak forming the boundary between the three countries. The park is accessible from the Honduran side, but only with difficulty. One local forestry officer's advice for accessing it was, "Take a bus into El Salvador, where buses go up to within a few minutes' walk of the peak"—a sentiment fairly widely echoed by locals. Clearly, the concept of actually walking up the mountain is not big in Montecristo. From the top, you can see the Pacific on a clear day. Pablo Rosas and his brother in Las Hojas are two reliable guides. A small cabin in the forest set up by Plan Trifinio is available for use, and Pablo has the key. If you decide to heed local advice and head into El Salvador, go to the town of Metapán, where there is a visitors center, a small museum, and guides available. Birders might especially be interested in the park, as over 275 species of birds have been recorded in the area.

The topographical map covering the Honduran portion of the park is *Montecristo 2359 III*.

www.moon.com

DESTINATIONS | ACTIVITIES | BLOGS | MAPS | BOOKS

MOON.COM is ready to help plan your next trip! Filled with fresh trip ideas and strategies, author interviews, informative travel blogs, a detailed map library, and descriptions of all the Moon guidebooks, Moon.com is all you need to get out and explore the world—or even places in your own backyard. While at Moon.com, sign up for our monthly e-newsletter for updates on new releases, travel tips, and expert advice from our on-the-go Moon authors. As always, when you travel with Moon, expect an experience that is uncommon and truly unique.

KEEP UP WITH MOON ON FACEBOOK AND TWITTER
JOIN THE MOON PHOTO GROUP ON FLICKR

MAP SYMBOLS

▬▬	Expressway	🄲	Highlight	✈	Airfield	⚓	Golf Course
▬▬	Primary Road	○	City/Town	✈	Airport	🅿	Parking Area
▬▬	Secondary Road	◉	State Capital	▲	Mountain	▲	Archaeological Site
▭ ▭ ▭	Unpaved Road	✸	National Capital	✚	Unique Natural Feature	⛪	Church
- - - -	Trail	★	Point of Interest				
⋯⋯⋯	Ferry	•	Accommodation	🌊	Waterfall	⛽	Gas Station
⋯⋯⋯	Railroad	▼	Restaurant/Bar	⏏	Park	〰	Glacier
▬▬	Pedestrian Walkway	■	Other Location	🚩	Trailhead	🌿	Mangrove
⊥⊥⊥⊥	Stairs	⋀	Campground	⛷	Skiing Area	▓	Reef
						░	Swamp

CONVERSION TABLES

°C = (°F − 32) / 1.8
°F = (°C x 1.8) + 32
1 inch = 2.54 centimeters (cm)
1 foot = 0.304 meters (m)
1 yard = 0.914 meters
1 mile = 1.6093 kilometers (km)
1 km = 0.6214 miles
1 fathom = 1.8288 m
1 chain = 20.1168 m
1 furlong = 201.168 m
1 acre = 0.4047 hectares
1 sq km = 100 hectares
1 sq mile = 2.59 square km
1 ounce = 28.35 grams
1 pound = 0.4536 kilograms
1 short ton = 0.90718 metric ton
1 short ton = 2,000 pounds
1 long ton = 1.016 metric tons
1 long ton = 2,240 pounds
1 metric ton = 1,000 kilograms
1 quart = 0.94635 liters
1 US gallon = 3.7854 liters
1 Imperial gallon = 4.5459 liters
1 nautical mile = 1.852 km

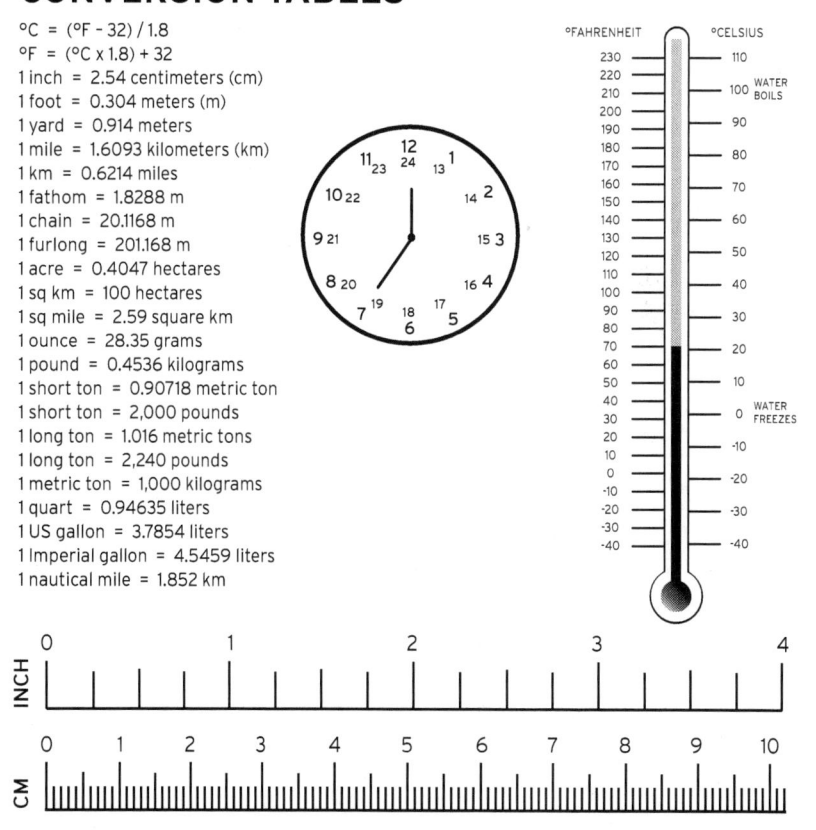

MOON SPOTLIGHT COPÁN
Avalon Travel
a member of the Perseus Books Group
1700 Fourth Street
Berkeley, CA 94710, USA
www.moon.com

Editor: Elizabeth Hollis Hansen
Series Manager: Kathryn Ettinger
Copy Editor: Ann Seifert
Graphics and Production Coordinator: Lucie Ericksen
Cover Designer: Kathryn Osgood
Map Editor: Kat Bennett
Cartographers: Andrea Butkovic, Heather Sparks, Chris Henrick
Proofreader: Natalie Mortensen

ISBN-13: 978-1-61238-363-7

Text © 2012 by Amy E. Roberts.
Maps © 2012 by Avalon Travel.
All rights reserved.

Some photos and illustrations are used by permission and are the property of the original copyright owners.

Front cover photo: detail of ancient Mayan carvings at Copán ruins © Holger Mette / istockphoto.com

Title page photo: the Acropolis at the ruins of Copán
© Amy E. Robertson

Printed in the United States.

Moon Spotlight and the Moon logo are the property of Avalon Travel. All other marks and logos depicted are the property of the original owners. All rights reserved. No part of this book may be translated or reproduced in any form, except brief extracts by a reviewer for the purpose of a review, without written permission of the copyright owner.

All recommendations, including those for sights, activities, hotels, restaurants, and shops, are based on each author's individual judgment. We do not accept payment for inclusion in our travel guides, and our authors don't accept free goods or services in exchange for positive coverage.

Although every effort was made to ensure that the information was correct at the time of going to press, the author and publisher do not assume and hereby disclaim any liability to any party for any loss or damage caused by errors, omissions, or any potential travel disruption due to labor or financial difficulty, whether such errors or omissions result from negligence, accident, or any other cause.

KEEPING CURRENT

If you have a favorite gem you'd like to see included in the next edition, or see anything that needs updating, clarification, or correction, please drop us a line. Send your comments via email to feedback@moon.com, or use the address above.

ABOUT THE AUTHOR

Amy E. Robertson

Hiking with her kids in jungles and cloud forests and lollygagging with the locals on the powdery beaches of the Cayos Cochinos are among Amy E. Robertson's favorite memories of nearly five years spent in Honduras. Amy and her family enjoyed exploring the mountain villages, Mayan ruins, white-sand beaches, and lush forests of Central America.

Amy is a Seattle native who has long been obsessed with travel. She studied in Boston and Madrid for her bachelor's degree, and upon graduating took a job with an international consulting firm. This position led Amy to a life of globetrotting — she traveled to more than 50 countries in less than three years. She then returned to school, earning a master's degree in development studies at the London School of Economics, where she also met her husband, who hails from Italy.

After working in international aid for five years in New York City, Amy and her family began life as expats in Ecuador, brought there by her husband's job with the United Nations. While in Ecuador, Amy made the career switch from development to travel writing, a livelihood she continued when she and her family made the move to Honduras in 2007. Her writing has since been published in *National Geographic Traveler*, *Christian Science Monitor*, and *Travel + Leisure*, among others.

Amy currently lives with her husband and two young children in Beirut, Lebanon. She spends three months a year divided among her family's hometowns: Seattle, Rome, and Messina, Sicily.